BLESSED BE PAIN!

Lessons on Sickness and Suffering from St Josemaría Escrivá

SINAG-TALA PUBLISHERS • MAKATI
SCEPTER PUBLISHERS • STRONGSVILLE, OH

Sinag-tala Publishers

This English edition is published in the Philippines by Sinag-tala Publishers, 6F, Loubel Bldg., San Antonio Village 1203 Makati City; and in the United States by Scepter Publishers, PO Box 360694, Strongsville, Ohio 44136.

For purposes of brevity, this English edition specifically omitted personages, articles, events and references which were cited or included in the original Spanish edition. Though significant and noteworthy, they are better explained in earlier publications on the history of Opus Dei and the life of its founder St. Josemaría Escrivá.

ISBN 978-971-554-233-3 (Sinag-tala Publishers)
ISBN 978-1-59417-375-2 (Scepter Publishers)

Miguel A. Monge (ed.)
[San Josemaría y los enfermos. English]
Blessed Be Pain! Lesson on Sickness and Suffering from St Josemaría Escrivá /Edited by Miguel A. Monge. Translation by Oliver C. Rojales. Edited and adapted by Ardella Crawford of Crawford Editing & Consulting, PA, USA.
pages cm
Includes bibliographical references.
Translation of: *San Josemaría y los enfermos.*
ISBN 978-1-59417-375-2 (pbk.:alk.paper) 1. Escrivá, Josemaría, 1902-1975. 2. Catholic Church—Spain—Clergy—Biography. 3. Opus Dei (Society) I. Title.

Contents

PREFACE

This book was primarily written to portray the great love which St. Josemaría had for the sick and the suffering, as well as his concern for doctors and health professionals, whom he admired for their total dedication to their patients. For St. Josemaría, the sick and sickness were a source of grace and strength for Christians and their work. His affirmation, "Blessed be pain!" may surprise many, but it reveals his vision of the Cross—and by extension, all crosses—as the place where all sufferings may be united to those of Christ. In this way, all who suffer may become co-redeemers with Christ.

Chapter 1 shows that St. Josemaría himself lived what he believed—and what the Church and other saints teaches—about pain and suffering. Chapter 2, though replete with technical terms, is perhaps the most pivotal in terms of the meaning of this book, for it calls to mind the words attributed to St. Francis: "Preach the gospel at all times. If necessary, use words." It presents an overview of the medical aspects of St. Josemaría's life, demonstrating that St. Josemaría himself suffered sickness in his own body for more than half of his life. Thus, it was out of his own experience that he could offer this loving advice: "When you are sick, offer with love your sufferings and they will be converted into incense that rises in honor of God and sanctifies you."

Chapter 3 presents the teachings and St. Josemaría's conviction that the sick and sickness are a source of grace and strength for the Christian. His vision of sickness transcended the merely physical and was founded on the purest love of Christ, whose image he saw in the sick and suffering. He viewed the sick, in their close identification with Christ, as being favored by God; hence one should attend to the sick discretely, consoling them because in this way, one also succeeds in uplifting his own spiritual life. Chapter 4 records memoirs and personal testimonies of medical practitioners who knew and dealt with St. Josemaría sometime in their lives.

Finally, the reading here is intended to be inspirational, a spiritual help to those who are sick or suffering in any way—which is to say, to all—because all mankind encounters sickness and suffering in life. "Man," says Job, "is born to trouble as the sparks fly upward." St. Josemaría quotes St. Teresa of Avila when he remarks, "Life is a bad night in a bad inn." Yet we are made for joy, the true joy that pours forth only from the side of our wounded Lord on the Cross.

May all who read this book find themselves drawn ever closer to Christ, "who, for the joy that was set before Him, endured the cross, despising the shame, and is seated at the right hand of the throne of God."

Chapter 1

Pain as Perceived by St. Josemaría and the Saints*

Blessed be pain... loved be pain...
sanctified be pain... glorified be pain!
The Way, 208

Pain: absurd or salvific?

The accusation of masochism comes easily to St. Josemaría's words "*Blessed be pain*", as though these words affirm that the greater and more intense the suffering, the greater will be the joy of the one who suffers. A current expression being used to refer to a positive portrayal of pain or suffering is severe pain ("*dolorismo*"). Before, one spoke also of the victim complex (*victimismo*) or offering oneself as a victim soul.[1] These terms are synonymous, more or less.

'Severe pain' can be understood as "perverse satisfaction through pain." St. Teresa Benedicta of the Cross (Edith

* This article was written by Miguel A. Monge who was the Chaplaincy Director at the University Clinic of the University of Navarre at that time.

[1] Certainly, St. Josemaría neither liked the word *victimismo* nor its content. Curiously, however, at some point in his life, he asked God to send him a serious illness in order to expiate and make reparation. Cfr. Vázquez de Prada, A., *The founder of Opus Dei*, Scepter Publishers, NY. p. 314.

Stein) points out that one can certainly fall into such seeking of suffering, but in that case, it would not be "a matter of spiritual aspiration, but a desire for a sensation, not better than other passions, but much worse for being against nature." This holy martyr explains the true meaning of love that suffering has, which, in the language of spiritual theologians, has been designated as expiation: "only he whose eyes of the spirit are open to the supernatural meaning of the happenings of this world, can aspire for expiation: this turns out [to be] possible only for men in whom the Spirit of Christ lives, that as members of the head, find in him life, strength, meaning, and direction."[2]

St John Paul II, in the Apostolic Letter *Salvifici doloris*, recognizes that pain, being absurd in itself, becomes salvific only when it is accepted and offered to Jesus Christ: "Faith in sharing in the suffering of Christ brings with it the interior certainty that the suffering person 'completes what is lacking in Christ's afflictions'; the certainty that in the spiritual dimension of the work of Redemption *he is serving*, like Christ, *the salvation of his brothers and sisters.* Therefore he is carrying out an irreplaceable service."[3]

Among the diverse commentaries to this Apostolic Letter, Pope Emeritus Benedict XVI, says: "Pain which is accepted and borne in communion with Christ, crucified and resurrected, finds a profound meaning for the person and for others; even more, it can be converted into a force for cure. This is not a theological speculation but an authentically realistic position, since a program that does not help man in suffering, but promises to suppress it completely, lacks realism."[4]

[2] Stein, E. (Teresa Benedicta of the Cross), *Science of the Cross*, Mt. Carmel, p. 145.

[3] Exhort. Ap. *Salvici doloris*, n. 27

[4] Cfr: Lozano Barragán, J., Theology and Medicine. Mexican Insti-

In another message, Pope Emeritus Benedict XVI said: If every man is our brother, much more must the sick, the suffering and those in need of care be at the centre of our attention, so that none of them feels forgotten or marginalized; indeed, 'the true measure of humanity is essentially determined in relationship to suffering and to the sufferer. This holds true both for the individual and for society. A society unable to accept its suffering members and incapable of helping to share their suffering and to bear it inwardly through "com-passion" is a cruel and inhuman society.' Dear sick and suffering, it is precisely through the wounds of Christ that we are able to see, with eyes of hope, all the evils that afflict humanity. In rising again, the Lord did not remove suffering and evil from the world, but he defeated them at their root. He opposed the arrogance of Evil with the omnipotence of his Love. He has shown us, therefore, that the way of peace and joy is Love: "Just as I have loved you, you also should love one another" (Jn 13:34). Christ, victor over death, is alive in our midst. And while with St. Thomas we also say "My Lord and my God!", let us follow our Master in readiness to spend our lives for our brothers and sisters (cfr. 1 Jn 3:16), becoming messengers of a joy that does not fear pain, the joy of the Resurrection.[5]"

For those prejudiced against pain, certainly many affirmations of Holy Scripture could be considered equally as masochistic, starting with the radical demand of Christ: "If anyone wants to come after me, let him deny himself, take up his cross and follow me" (Lk 9:23). But if taking the cross or accepting the pain that it includes is synonymous to being an imitator of Christ, the cross cannot constitute a disgrace, a misfortune; on the contrary, it can be—it is—a blessing, a

tute of Social Christian Doctrine, México 2000, p. 64.

[5] Excerpt from the Message of Benedict XVI for the 19th World Day of the Sick 2010.

triumph.[6] Thus, the Fathers of the Church testify together with the testimony of a multitude of saints, as is verified in so many praiseworthy affirmations of the cross that appear in their writings. St John Paul II teaches, "the saints have lived through something similar to the experience of Jesus on the cross, in the paradoxical confluence of joy and sorrow." He turns to two testimonies:[7]

a) "God the Father showed St. Catherine of Siena how joy can be united with suffering in holy souls: 'And the soul is happy and suffering: suffering for the sins of his neighbor, happy for the union and affection of charity that he has received in himself. They imitate the immaculate Lamb, my only begotten Son, who being on the Cross was happy and suffering.'"[8]

b) In like manner the Pope gave testimony on St. Therese de Lisieux, "who lives through her agony in communion with that of Jesus who is happy and in anguish"[9]: St. Therese said, "Our Lord in the Garden of Olives enjoyed all the joys of the Trinity; nevertheless, his agony was no less cruel. It is a mystery, but I assure you that from what I experienced myself, I understand something."[10] St John

[6] Cfr. Mateo-Seco, F. L., Wisdom of the Cross. The Mystery of the Cross in the Writings of Josemaria Escrivá. Scripta Theologica 24 (1992) 419-438.

[7] Apostolic Letter *Novo millennio ineunte,* January 6, 2001, n. 27.

[8] *Dialogue of Divine Providence*, n. 78.

[9] *Novo millennio ineunte*, n. 27.

[10] Last conversations. Yellow notebook, July 6, 1897: Complete Works, Vatican 1997, 1003. Cfr. also: "The thought of an earthly happiness does not give me any joy, but rather I ask myself sometimes, how will it be possible to be happy without suffering? Jesus, no doubt, will change my nature; but on the contrary, I will miss suffering and the valley of tears."

Paul II concludes his reflection thus: "Jesus cry on the cross is not the cry of anguish of a man without hope, but the prayer of the Son who offers his life to the Father in love, for the salvation of all."[11] Even the testimony of some poets—*"palabra verdadera"*—confirms it:

Paul Claudel said, "God did not come to suppress suffering or to explain it. He came to fill it with his presence. Many things remain obscure: but here is one thing at least that we cannot say to God: You do not know what it is to suffer."[12]

Another Spanish poet León Felipe expresses the same thing with broken, almost violent tones:[13]

You came to glorify the tears...
not to wipe them away...
You came to open the wounds...
not to close them...
You came to light the bonfire...
not to extinguish them...
You came to say:
Let fire, blood, tears flow...
Like water!

[11] *Novo millennio ineunte,* n. 26. Similar expressions can be found in other texts of the Magisterium: "It is an especially Christian idea to see in pain a sign of the love of God and a source of graces": Pius XII, Aloc. 17 July 1940. Or this other one of John Paul II: Suffering "is something good, before which the Church bows down in reverence with all the depth of her faith in the Redemption". Ap. Exh. *Salvifici doloris,* n. 24.

[12] Quoted in Gafo, J., Euthanasia, the law of a dignified death, Ed. Themes of Today, Madrid 1989, p. 22.

[13] León Felipe, *Antología Rota,* Losada, 3rd ed., Barcelona 1970, p. 35.

Devotion to the Virgin of Almudena

In his usual journeys on foot throughout Madrid, St Josemaría has the custom of greeting the images of Our Lady that he will encounter along the way. He had a special devotion to the image of the Virgin of Almudena, patroness of Madrid, which was in a niche in the Cuesta de la Vega. Before her, more than once, he was seen kneeling and praying in the middle of the street.

This was the constant teaching of St. Josemaría who always highlighted the positive aspects of the cross: "The way of our personal sanctification passes, daily, through the Cross: this way is not unfortunate, because Christ himself helps us, and with Him sadness cannot co-exist. *In laetitia nulla dies sine cruce!* (With joy, no day without a cross) I like to repeat; with the soul pierced with joy, no day without a Cross."[14] The following text is also relevant: "Let us not forget that in all human activities there must be men and women who, in their lives and work, raise Christ's Cross aloft for all to see, as an act of reparation. It is a symbol of peace and of joy, a symbol of the Redemption and of the unity of the human race. It is a symbol of the love that the Most Holy Trinity, God the Father, God the Son, and God the Holy Spirit had, and continues to have, for mankind."[15]

[14] Cfr. Celaya, I. de, *Unidad de vida y plenitud cristiana*, en AA.VV., *Mons. Josemaría Escrivá* y el Opus Dei, Eunsa, Pamplona 1985, p. 337.
[15] *Furrow*, no. 985.

From what has been said, we understand why St. Josemaría would repeat frequently that Opus Dei had been born among the poor and the abandoned sick of the hospitals in Madrid and that thanks to the prayer and suffering of those persons offered to God, he could continue in the task that God had entrusted to him.[16]

Severe pain

However, there are authors who try to correct these approaches which are referred to as 'severe pain' (*doloristas*). They essentially exclude existence itself from the pain within the divine plan, avoiding, but not denying its positive dimension. Though they undoubtedly have good intentions, they try to solve the problem by saying: "Jesus taught that God does not send evil to anyone: neither to the just nor to sinners. He only sends what is good." In the face of the obstacle of pain in the life of men, they do not attribute it to the will of God but look for other explanations.

But this does not solve the problem. Pain exists and needs an explanation. Pain is part of life. Its occurrence is both common and mysterious, above all with reference to its meaning. And if it exists,[17] it must mean something

[16] In the Cathedral of Almudena in Madrid, there is a beautiful memento of this. In the side chapel dedicated to St. Josemaría, the bas-reliefs depict the links of St. Josemaría with Madrid. One shows him praying in the Cuesta de la Vega before the image of the Virgin of Almudena, and another shows him consoling a sick person. The second relief is explained thus: "In order to fulfill the mission that God entrusted to him, he also sought the help of pain, working heroically for many years, in the hospitals and isolated barrios to the extent that he could affirm that Opus Dei was born among the poor and sick of Madrid...".

[17] There are many types of pain. What should interest us and what is really fearsome, is that which breaks man from within, what seems to be meaningless and without explanation. We are referring

in the plan of Creation and Redemption,[18] although one tries—and one should always try—to eliminate or at least attenuate it.[19] But in one way or the other, pain and sickness are always present in the life of men. But what should we do? Mere conformity is not enough, as if it were a matter of inexorable fate: "Do not yield to the temptation of considering pain as a negative experience only," John Paul II warns.[20] We have to recognize the fact that pain in itself is an evil and as such cannot be loved. When we talk of the redeeming death of Christ, we understand that we have not been redeemed through pain itself, but through an infinite love that has been manifested in the acceptance of suffering. For this reason, the acceptance of pain and privation on the part of a Christian is not directed, as is logical, to suffering in itself—that is, to the cross in itself—but to Him who has been crucified on it.[21] "Human suffering receives expiatory efficacy," Edith Stein says, "only if it is

to unexpected sufferings which penetrate deeply into one's soul, such as an act of terrorism (remember what happened on September 11, 2001 in New York or on March 11, 2004 in Madrid?), the death of a loved one, a serious illness, calumny, imprisonment, etc.

[18] Simple people understand the presence of pain as a constituent part of life. African culture expresses it very well. A Kenyan woman in agony was saying before she died of cancer: "When one is born and when one dies, he has to suffer a little. Pain is 'a thing of God'; and I am looking at him in my last sorrow. I am alone with Him." Cfr. Toranzo, E.; Okondo, B.: Waithire, L., *Deja que África te Hable,* Rialp, Madrid 1997, p. 108.

[19] In this sense, St Josemaría used to say: "Physical pain, when it can be removed, is removed. There are enough sufferings in life! And when it cannot be removed, it is offered up." Herranz, G., *Sin miedo a la vida y sin miedo a la muerte.* This is besides the task of medicine, which has achieved impressive developments in this field, i.e., modern pain management units in many hospitals.

[20] Cfr. *Mensaje para la Jornada Mundial del Enfermo,* Fátima 1997: "Ecclesia" 2882-2883 (1997) 47-48.

[21] Burggraf, J., *Divine Filiation, in Santidad y Mundo: Estudios en Torno a Las Enseñanzas del Beato Josemaría Escrivá,* EUNSA, Pamplona 1996, p. 123.

united to the suffering of the divine head"[22] because without union with the cross—or, more accurately, with the Christ crucified on it—there is no fecundity in Christian life, since *"pain is the touchstone of Love,"* as St. Josemaría affirmed.[23] Some people consider pain simply as an error in the divine plan of Creation, and that the death of Christ on the cross is a consequence of human evil (the fanaticism and the hatred of the Pharisees), rather than the fruit of a will expressed openly by Christ. But this means ignoring the true meaning of the cross. As St. Paul notes: "For the doctrine of the cross is foolishness to those who perish, but to those who are saved, that is, to us, it is the power of God" (1 Cor. 1:18). The Apostle shows that true wisdom comes from God, and it has been manifested on the cross of Christ. On the cross are fulfilled the words of Isaias 24:14, which St. Paul quotes as follows: "I will destroy the wisdom of the wise and reject the prudence of the prudent." Simplicity and humility are necessary in order to penetrate into the divine wisdom of the cross. Edith Stein would say, as mentioned earlier, that this can be understood only by men in whom the Spirit of Christ dwells.[24]

Joy in Suffering

St Josemaría combined both love and suffering in his life in a way that he found "joy in suffering": "My way is to love and to suffer. But love makes me find joy in suffering, to the extent that now it seems impossible for me to suffer anymore. I already said it: no one can upset me. In addition, I say: there is no one who can make me suffer, because suffering gives me joy and peace" (24-I-1932).[25] From the beginning he knew how to transmit this spirit to his spiri-

[22] *Science of the Cross*, o.c., p. 146.

[23] St Josemaría Escrivá, *The Way*, n. 439.

[24] *Science of the Cross, o.c.*, p. 145.

[25] *Intimate Notes*, n. 582; in Vázquez de Prada, A., *o.c.*, I, pp. 418-419.

tual children. He gives a moving account of the sickness of María Ignacia Escobar, one of the first women members of Opus Dei:[26] "That sister of ours loves the will of God. She sees in those long, painful and many illnesses (there is not a healthy bone in her body), the blessings of Jesus, and, while affirming in her humility that she deserves punishment, she sees the terrible pain she is feeling in her whole system, especially on account of the abdominal adhesions, not as a punishment, but of mercy."[27]

On another occasion while doing his prayer aloud, he makes this affirmation: "Lord, you made me understand that to have the Cross is to find happiness, joy. And the reason—I see it with more clarity—is this: to have the Cross is to identify oneself with Christ, it is to be Christ, and therefore, to be a son of God."[28] Some words of St. Paul constitute the last stages of the spiritual itinerary of a Christian in relation to suffering: "I rejoice now in the sufferings I bear for your sake; and what is lacking of the sufferings of Christ, I fill up in my flesh for his body, which is the Church" (Col. 1:24). Take note that the joy in the presence of pain is being happy to suffer for Christ.

Taking all these into consideration, we see that in the absence of any intense life of piety, a soul is just at the initial stage. It would not be prudent to insist on those aspects of pain if he has not yet began a life of piety. Based on my experience as hospital chaplain, it is not advisable

[26] María Ignacia was born in Hornachuelos (Córdoba) and joined Opus Dei in 1932. She died in the King's Hospital in Madrid of tuberculosis on September 13, 1933: Cfr. Cejas, J.M., *La paz y la alegría*, Rialp, Madrid 2001.

[27] *Intimate Notes*, n. 1006; quoted by Vázquez de Prada, A., *o.c.*, I, p. 440.

[28] Cfr. Rodríguez, P., Omnia traham ad meipsum. En sentido de Juan 12, 32 *en La Experiencia Espiritual de Mons. Escrivá "Romana" 1991*, pp. 331-352.

The Death of Maria Ignacia

On September 13 1933, one of the first women members of Opus Dei, Maria Ignacia Escobar, died. St Josemaría remained by her side up to her last moments, assisting her to die in a holy way.

however to suggest such optimistic considerations on pain when a sick person does not have a deep interior life—the fruit of God's grace and many years of struggle—because he will not be able to comprehend it. St. Josemaría deplores the lack of preparation of some persons: "There is a kind of fear around, a fear of the Cross, of our Lord's Cross. What has happened is that people have begun to regard as crosses all the unpleasant things that crop up in life, and they do not know how to take them as God's children should, with supernatural outlook. So much so that they are even removing the roadside crosses set up by our forefathers...!"[29]

On another occasion, he says more forcefully: "The Cross is still a symbol of death instead of becoming a sign of life. One still flees from the cross as if it were the gallows when it is a throne of glory. There are still Christians who reject the Cross and identify it with pain, instead of identifying it with love. You and I—he was telling his children—have to look for the Cross, to look for it—let us understand each other—in order to love it, in order to receive it with open arms, when it comes [...] A Cross, from which He reigns: *oportet illum regnare* (cfr. 1 Cor. 15:25) from which He shows Himself great, great, great, very great, eternal, immense, majestic, victorious. And we are small, *illum oportet crescere, me autem minui* (Jn 3:30). My children,

[29] *Way of the Cross*, 5.

you have the personal experience that the Father is not deceiving you. I have told you and I have written many times what I have experienced in my poor life: pain is not pain when we embrace it in union with Jesus. The Cross is not something from which one has to flee but something that one has to receive with love. And then the Cross is that of Christ, He carries it and, therefore, it is not heavy. That is why I am somewhat annoyed when they talk so much—you will tell me that it is the usual way of saying things in asceticism and you may be right—of the cross, of crosses... but it does not convince me. Lord, no, no, no! In the spirit of Opus Dei, the Cross and crosses are joy, they are honor, they are progress, perfection, sanctity. Joy here and victory there![30]

Really, it is only possible to cry out 'Blessed be pain!' when one sees in the cross, in all the crosses, a participation in the Passion of Christ, where the soul identifies itself with Christ and becomes a co-redeemer.[31] Meanwhile, looking for simple and adequate explanations about pain, one should help the sick take upon themselves the proportionate part of suffering of which they are capable of. More than human arguments—which become dry and can be rejected most of the time—one should try to make those souls encounter the suffering of Christ on the Cross, since the one who teaches—the true Teacher—is the crucified

[30] St J. Escrivá, AGP, P18, pp. 255-256.

[31] "In the face of the reality of pain, the remedy is to look at Christ": Cfr. Echevarría, J., *Itinerarios de Vida Cristiana*, Planeta, Barcelona, 2000, p. 173. As hospital chaplain, I have had the following personal experience: many sick people, complaining about their situation, whom I encourage to look at—or to complain before—the image of Christ in the room, frequently feel moved; and as they reflect on the pains of Our Lord in his Passion, they consider theirs to be less severe.

Christ.[32] And we must remember that *"as long as we are on earth and have not yet arrived at the fullness of the future life, we can never have true love without sacrifice and pain. This pain becomes sweet and lovable; it is a source of interior joy. But it is an authentic pain, for it involves overcoming one's own selfishness and taking Love as the rule of each and everything we do."*[33] Pain continues to be a mystery, but with the death of Christ on the Cross it has become the touchstone of love. The terms pain, suffering, love and joy—apparently contradictory to one another—all blend harmoniously in the Christian soul. We see that only from the love of Jesus Christ, who voluntarily gave himself up on the Cross for us, and from faith in the eternal life, can men enter the mystery of pain. It ceases to be a contradiction and is rather converted into a trial that one undergoes to reach interior maturity and to meet our Father God in eternal life.[34] Indeed it is a matter of accepting, always and in everything, the will of God: "only thus will we taste the sweetness of Christ's Cross, and come to embrace it with all the strength of love."[35] Recourse to Christ is the key to overcome the contradictions of life. Only by being united to the suffering of Christ on the Cross can we find happiness amidst adversity.

[32] St Josemaría, Christ is Passing By, Sinag-tala Publishers, Makati 1974, n. 43.

[33] We dealt with this question thoroughly in Monge, M.A. and León, J. L., *The Sense of Suffering*, Palabra, 3rd ed., Madrid 2002.

[34] St Josemaría, *Way of the Cross*, IV Station, p. 50.

[35] Edith Stein also explains: "Human suffering receives its expiatory strength only when it is united to the suffering of the divine head. To suffer and to be happy in suffering, to be on earth and go through its dirty and rough roads and, even so, to reign with Christ at the right hand of the Father; to laugh and cry with the children of this world, and to sing praises to God with the choirs of angels without interruption: this is the life of the Christian until that day when dawn breaks into eternity." *Science of the Cross*, Mt Carmel, o.c., p. 146.

Javier Echevarria, as Prelate, remembers some words which he heard straight from the lips of St. Josemaría, summarizing what we want to recall here: *"In Opus Dei, if we live the spirit that the Lord has wanted for us, suffering is converted into love, and into love with joy. Do not forget, the time will come when I will have gone to account to God, and you will be able to repeat to your brothers what you heard me say that when suffering comes, we will love, bless and convert it into a means to give glory to God, always with joy, which does not mean that it is not difficult... When sickness comes, we have to love it, and we have to know how to sanctify it because it is "the professional work" which the Lord puts in those moments into our hands."*[36]

The misunderstandings provoked by the aforementioned expressions of St. Josemaría are similar to what happened with his other teachings, such as the universal call to sanctity, which at one time was considered heretical, but which has become part of the common patrimony of the Church with the passage of time.[37] In reality, the idea of the "glorification" of pain is not exactly original to Josemaría Escrivá; this teaching forms part of the spiritual tradition of the Catholic Church. It is enough to read the Fathers of the Church, St. Therese of Jesus, St. John of the Cross, St. Therese of Lisieux, and St. Benedicta of the Cross (Edith Stein), to name only a few, in order to verify that we are dealing with the same doctrine. What St. Josemaría

[36] Echevarría, J., *Memoria del Beato Josemaría,* o.c., p. 39.

[37] Referring to October 2, 1928, the foundational date of Opus Dei, Pedro Rodríguez comments, "As synthesis, we can say that St Josemaría 'discovers' the universal call of God to sanctity being fulfilled not only in extraordinary situations but in the heart of human work and of the most common circumstances of life, a calling which seems to him to have been 'forgotten' in the practice of Christians that is characterized mainly by the separation between faith and ordinary life." *The Way, Critical-historical edition,* o. c., p. 7.

managed to do was to assume and express in an outstanding way his own experience of pain in ordinary life and to transmit it to Christians who live their lives under similar ordinary circumstances.

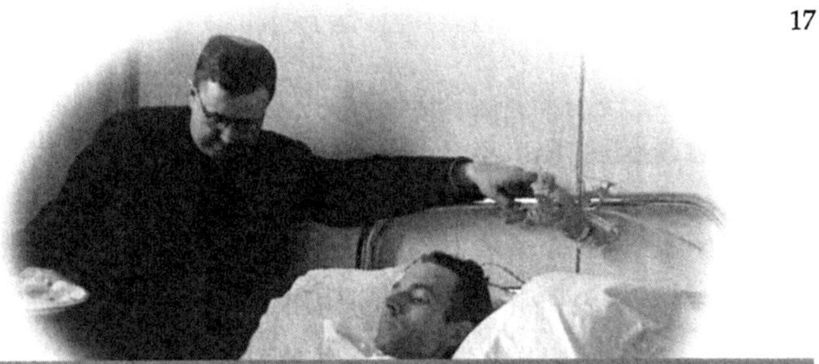

Chapter 2

Pain as Experienced by St. Josemaría*

> Cross, toil, anguish:
> such will be your lot as long as you live.
> That was the way Christ went,
> and the disciple is not above his Master.
>
> The Way, 699

Medical history

St. Josemaría's childhood demonstrates the usual family and child history of illnesses of that era (e.g., measles at the age of three), except for a serious infectious sickness—probably meningitis—at the age of two. In his youth and during the early years of his stay in Madrid, St. Josemaría experienced a series of disorders that we could call "minor"; these had a doubtful connection, or at least an indirect one, to his principal complaint and, in many cases,

* After an exhaustive physical examination of St Josemaría in Sepember 1966, Drs. Eduardo O. de Landazuri, Diego M. Caro and Jose M. Heras wrote his medical history, which serves as the basis of this narrative. Their report was included among the documents for the process of beatification of J. Escrivá.

Publisher's note: Dr. Eduardo Ortiz de Landazuri and his wife have both been named as Servants of God. His sister Guadalupe O. de Landazuri was recently beatified on May 18, 2019 in Madrid Spain. All three were members of Opus Dei.

were a direct consequence of the hardships he suffered before and during the civil war of 1936.

Between 1930 and 1936, as a consequence of an overly fatty diet, he weighed 90 kg or almost 200 pounds. Between 1936 and 1938, together with frequent colds and sore throats, he had several rheumatic outbreaks that affected his knees and other joints.

In 1937 and 1938 he had several episodes of respiratory infections in which he coughed up blood (hemoptysis), for which an exhaustive checkup could not determine the cause. During the Civil War between 1936 and 1939) his weight went down to 44 kg or approximately 97 pounds.

The fundamental illness that seriously affected his health, however, starting in 1940 was insulin-dependent diabetes (diabetes type 1), which manifested itself in four stages:

> 1. The latent stage or pre-diabetes between 1942 and 1943. There was no glucose in the urine, but he suffered certain symptoms of the sickness: much thirst along with abundant urination, fatigue, and weight gain. During that time his blood pressure was at the upper limit of normal (160/90).
>
> 2. Full-blown diabetes from 1943 to 1946. Sugar was present in the urine and was accompanied by weight loss, progressive malaise, and clearly abnormal blood pressure (190/90). His first treatment was in 1946 by Dr. J. Rof Carballo, who dissuaded him from making a trip to Rome which, nevertheless, he had to pursue in order to step up the process for the approval of Opus Dei by the Holy See.

3. Unbalanced diabetes, with the need for high doses of insulin (more than 100 units in 24 hours), first in Madrid, then in Rome (1946-1954). He frequently had infections on the skin, mouth, etc.

4. On April 27, 1954, St. Josemaría went into extremely severe shock in reaction to insulin. As the consequence of a change in the type of retardant insulin, he experienced a modest anaphylactic reaction on the first day of its application. On the third day, he went into an extraordinarily violent shock with a loss of consciousness, with intense reddening first and then extreme pallor in his face, and significant rigidity. When he recovered from the shock, the diabetes had disappeared, not only on the glucose content, but to the rest of the symptoms as well. From that moment on, he no longer required insulin.

Accompanying this metabolic picture were also occasional outbreaks of gout due to an increase of uric acid in the blood. As a result of diabetes, St. Josemaría developed kidney (renal) disease, and this resulted in renal insufficiency that deteriorated until the end of his life.

Initially both symptoms and alterations observed in the blood were slight. Symptoms of subsequent renal insufficiency appeared, with over-production of and a slight concentration in the urine, which developed slowly but continuously. This process, with its tendency to high blood pressure, resulted in hypertensive cardiopathy,[1] the heart

[1] The condition referred to here is weakening of the heart muscle as a result of high blood pressure. Early signs of the condition can be coughing, weakness, and shortness of breath; as the disease develops, there may be swelling in the legs, weight gain, and significant

condition that was the immediate cause of his death.

Around 1966, arteriosclerosis, more colloquially known as hardening of the arteries, was already evident, along with elevated cholesterol, which was later controlled at normal values but subsequently elevated in the last year. During a radiological checkup, arterial calcification could be observed in many places. Taking these conditions into account, the doctors thought it very probable that there were other vascular localizations of this process (coronary, retinian vessels and, logically, renal) that were not explored directly. However, the principal circulatory disorder was the hypertensive cardiopathy already mentioned, with an evident left ventricle hypertrophy. Despite the tendency toward a rise in blood pressure, it was not extraordinarily high.

The last datum in the medical history of St. Josemaría was the account of his death. It does not appear in the report, but an account comes from Msgr. Álvaro del Portillo in his letter of June 29, 1975, describing in detail the events of June 26:

> He celebrated the Holy Mass at 7:53 a.m. At 9:35 a.m. we left for Castelgandolfo... We arrived at about 10:30 a.m. accompanied by Javi [Msgr. Javier Echevarría] and by Javier Cotelo, who was driving, and by me [Msgr. Álvaro del Portillo].
>
> He started to talk to us... in that get-together which was short, less than twenty minutes.... A few minutes later... he started to feel tired.... The

episodes of shortness of breath, especially at night. This condition can end in congestive heart failure. The left ventricle hypertrophy referred to here is a thickening of the muscle in the left ventricular chamber of the heart, which is the heart's main pumping chamber.

> get-together ended...he rested a little.... Immediately, when it seemed like he had recovered, we left for Rome.... He was returning from Villa delle Rose,[2] undoubtedly tired, but serene and happy.... When he entered Bruno Buozzi (his permanent residence) a few minutes before 12 noon, he greeted the Lord with a paused genuflection.... Then we went up to the room where he usually worked, and a few seconds after entering he called "Javi!" Javier [Msgr. Javier Echevarría] had stayed behind in order to close the door of the lift...; and he repeated with more force: "Javi!" And afterwards in a weaker voice: "I don't feel well".... Suddenly... he collapsed on the floor.... Joe Soria (Dr José Luis Soria) and I were already in the room...
>
> It was an hour and a half of struggle, of hope: oxygen, injections, heart massages.... We took turns.... We could not believe that we were experiencing the moment of this very great sorrow..., and we continued trying to do the impossible.... We resisted the thought that he had passed away.... For us, it has been really a sudden death.

Given the conditions already mentioned, as well as the intensity of the onset and the absence of pain or other manifestations, St. Josemaría's doctors speculated that the cause of his death may have been malignant arrhythmia of the heart (ventricular fibrillation). When this occurs, the muscles of the ventricle, rather than contracting normally, merely quiver, so that no blood is pumped from the heart. Such can occur in patients with a tendency to hypokalemia, which is a potassium deficiency, because a po-

[2] Editor's Note: A center of Opus Dei in the "Castelli Romani" some 30 kilometers from the capital.

tassium imbalance adversely affects the muscles, including the heart muscle, and hypokalemia can arise from the taking of diuretics given as treatment for high blood pressure. It would appear that the crisis of ventricular fibrillation caused instantaneous cardiac arrest, more familiarly known as a heart attack.

Identification with the Divine Will

After this succinct summary of his clinical history, it is interesting to look into a clinical evaluation of the symptoms and signs caused by his sickness, as well as to explain the importance and seriousness of some of those clinical data and the contrast to what was the real life of St. Josemaría. The commentary on various periods of St. Josemaría's life can be derived from the previously mentioned medical documentation and biographical notes, to which his doctors were direct witnesses, or from firsthand information from Msgr. Álvaro del Portillo and Msgr. Javier Echevarría. The data, combined with eyewitness accounts, show how he lived detached from his biopathological situation, absolutely oblivious to the limitations proper to his sickness. Only he who would have known "from within"—that is, a doctor—the evolution and extent of his various illnesses, would have suspected the true state of his poor health, as the external manifestations were few. His conduct was absolutely normal, an expression of his naturalness and simplicity, because he knew how to downplay the diverse diseases or discomforts and to accept everything that Providence sent, as proof—also in infirmity—of, his identification with the divine will.[3]

[3] Referring to how he endured some dental pains as in this case, Msgr Echevarría writes: "Because of this, St. Josemaría Escrivá did not suffer the least complex or the least affliction. He offered it to the Lord and continued working and speaking as if nothing had happened, exerting the effort so that he could be understood. From

Álvaro del Portillo

Msgr Álvaro was the first successor of St. Josemaría as head of Opus Dei. He joined Opus Dei in 1935, during a spiritual retreat preached by St. Josemaría. Soon he became a faithful and close collaborator of the Founder, who as far back in 1939 called him "saxum," because he was hoping to rely on him to undertake the task of governing the Work. On June 25, 1944, he was ordained priest. In September of 1975 he was elected the first successor of St Josemaría; at that time, he was Secretary General of Opus Dei and had worked almost 40 years beside the Founder. On November 28, 1982, when the Holy Father established the Work as Personal Prelature, he also appointed Msgr Álvaro as Prelate of Opus Dei, and on January 6, 1991, he conferred on him the episcopal ordination. He died in Rome on March 23, 1994.

St. Josemaría suffered, as we have already seen, several serious diseases, real and objective, but he never had a "sickness complex." The typical psychological manifestations of someone who suffers chronic illnesses that deteriorate into more serious conditions appeared neither in his regimen of life nor in his external conduct.

Knowing these clinical and analytic data, the doctors who attended to him were astonished at how St. Josemaría conducted himself during all this time: his intense activity at the service of souls; the energy and vitality in his actions; the serene and cheerful spirit that he inspired in others; the exemplary exercise of serious obligations derived from his task of governing Opus Dei; the zeal that led him

the very outset, he adapted himself to the prosthesis, although these gave him very painful wounds which developed pus in the gums, lasting longer than usual." Cfr. *Memoria del Beato Josemaría Escrivá*, Rialp, Madrid 2000, p. 32.

Javier Echevarria

On April 20, 1994 he was elected Prelate of Opus Dei. Until then he had been Vicar General of the Prelature. Previously, he had collaborated for more than twenty years with the Founder of Opus Dei, at the side of Msgr Álvaro del Portillo. He died on December 12, 2016.

to commit himself to undertake arduous projects, thereby increasing the risks for his already weak health, although following always what doctors prescribed and what those around him advised.

Hardships after the civil war

In the detailed medical history gathered in September 1966 and in the medical checkup done during that time in the University Hospital, the doctors came to know the hardships of all types he had experienced in the years immediately before and during the civil war. On many occasions the lack of necessities for survival added to the insecurity that preceded an authentic persecution against his person and those closest to him. Among the after effects of this period of privations, what stands out above all is the development of his diabetic process. Having started in 1942-1943, it began, shortly after, to acquire signs of malignancy, as was apparent from the elevated levels of glucose in the blood and urine, and the significant doses of insulin necessary to attain compensation. The negative opinion of Dr. Rof Carballo when, in May 1946, he was consulted on the impending trip to Rome by the Founder also testifies to the seriousness of the diabetes.

During those more than ten years that the diabetes lasted, St. Josemaría worked as if he were completely healthy, overcoming intense and constant headaches, a habitual condition of very profound fatigue, frequent skin infections, double vision, etc. These were the years when Opus Dei, expanded first throughout Spain and later throughout Europe. This labor led him to travel continuously from one city and one country to another, under very difficult material conditions, in order to attend to the formation of the members and to carry out personally an intense apostolic activity with people of all classes and professions. In addition, he undertook what he called the juridical battle, which was necessary so that Opus Dei might be given a juridical status according to the spirit that he had received from God. The first outbreaks of the disease coincided, for example, with the beginning of the Priestly Society of the Holy Cross, which entailed much work. During this time strong material and spiritual contradictions intensified, provoked by those who did not understand Opus Dei and who raised calumnies before the ecclesiastical and civil authorities.

After 1946 and coinciding with his trip to Rome, his diabetes worsened, although this did not put a stop to his incessant activity. It was precisely during these years and those that followed when the Holy See granted pontifical approval to Opus Dei. During this time also the Work established, with grave financial difficulties, its Central Headquarters in Rome and started the construction of the Roman College of the Holy Cross, designed for the formation of members coming from countries in which the Work was already stable: Spain, Portugal, Italy, England, Ireland, France… and in America: Mexico, Argentina, the United States, Chile, Venezuela, Peru, Guatemala.

Priestly Society of the Holy Cross

Editor's Note: The Priestly Society of the Holy Cross was founded by St. Josemaría on February 14, 1943. According to the Statutes it is "a clerical association proper and intrinsic to the Prelature in such manner that with it, the Prelature forms a unique whole and from it, it cannot be separated"; it comprises those faithful of Opus Dei who receive priestly ordination (which constitute the presbyterum of the Prelature) and to which can be associated also priests and deacons incardinated in the particular Churches that continue maintaining the strictest relation of dependence on their own bishops.

On April 27, 1954, after the very serious anaphylactic shock already described, the diabetic symptoms disappeared completely, and in the urine and blood tests—done innumerable times after that date—the signs of diabetes were never found. It is true, however, that signs of lesions in the ocular, renal, and cardiovascular organs and systems remained.

The summary of the medical exam of September 1966 does show slight evidence of disease of the blood vessels (hypertensive angiopathy) with ocular, cardiovascular, and renal manifestations, all with relatively benign characteristics.

Circumstances after Vatican Council II

In the period between September 1966 and March 1972, the deterioration in renal function became apparent. Levels of cholesterol and uric acid were also high, and St. Josemaría suffered from calcium deficiency (hypocalcemia). On one occasion he was experiencing a serious round of gout, with intense pain and inflammation of the great ar-

Opus Dei as a Personal Prelature

Editor's Note: The actions taken by the Founder of Opus Dei in Rome soon started to give fruits: the letter *"Brevis sane,"* on August 13, 1946, was in praise of the ends of Opus Dei. A little later, the promulgation of the Apostolic Constitution *Provida Mater Ecclesia* created the figure of the Secular Institutes, and Opus Dei could accommodate itself to that new juridical form, which was not completely adequate to its charisma, but which allowed it to have a supra-diocesan government and to emphasize more its unity and universality. Pius XII approved Opus Dei as a Secular Institute with the *Decretum laudis,* which goes with the title *Primum Institutum,* on February 24, 1947. On June 16, 1950, through the Decree *Primum Inter,* Pius XII granted Opus Dei definitive approval as a Secular Institute with pontifical right. On November 28, 1982, John Paul II erected Opus Dei as a personal prelature of universal scope, with its own statutes. Thus, the definitive juridical solution that St Josemaría had wanted was obtained, seconding the divine will; and so the juridical itinerary that had lasted for many years was concluded. (Cfr. Requena, F. M. and Sesé, J., *Fuentes para la Historia del Opus Dei,* o.c., pp. 89 and 159.)

ticulations (knee, elbow, etc.); he was completely immobile from these symptoms, and to these were added very painful cramps caused by the calcium deficiency. He could not stand up and had to be practically carried, since he could not move a step. Also in November 1971 the first nocturnal crisis of cardiac dyspnea (shortness of breath) appeared with tightness and pain in the chest, occasioned by a rise in blood pressure along with left ventricular failure.

During this period, St. Josemaría's response in the face of these limitations of health was to work without pause or rest, complying with the medical prescriptions, but without giving in to the least exception in his lifestyle. These years coincided with his profound sorrow concerning the difficult situation in the Church arising from some people's arbitrary application of the directives of the Second Vatican Council. Under these circumstances, St. Josemaría redoubled his self-surrender. He constantly took measures to ensure the doctrinal formation of his children and expanded his personal apostolate even more.

In 1967, for example, he presided in Pamplona over the Second Assembly of Friends of the University of Navarre, in which he celebrated the Holy Mass and preached a homily (published afterwards with the title "Passionately Loving the World")[4] before many thousands of people. In those days he had very numerous meetings—"get-togethers," he called them—which required intense effort on his part.

In those years he traveled through Italy, Switzerland, France, Germany, Austria, Belgium, Holland, Spain, and Portugal in order to visit different Marian shrines and to do pastoral work with thousands of souls. Likewise, he went to Italy in 1967 and to Mexico in 1970, where he did priestly work for 40 days, traveling through the interior of the country and overcoming difficulties caused by the climate, altitude, etc.

It was also during this time that he gave a boost to the beginning of the School of Theology of the University of Navarre and to the creation of a very wide range of apostolic undertakings and social projects everywhere. St. Josemaría's therapeutic plan was aimed at lowering his levels of uric acid and cholesterol, avoiding weight gain, trying to prevent infections so that protein catabolism would not

[4] Editor's Note: The homily is included in *Conversations with Msgr. Escrivá*, Sinag-tala Publishers Makati, pp. 221-235.

increase, recommending an abundant intake of liquids and assuring that he could lead a normal lifestyle—or, to be more precise, what was normal for St. Josemaría—i.e., characterized by intense daily work.

Neither his profound fatigue nor his many nights of insomnia kept him from carrying out the immense task described here.

Catechesis in Spain and Portugal

Between April 1972 and January 1974, St. Josemaría's renal insufficiency gradually worsened; this development may have been caused partly by the bilateral pneumonia that he suffered in Pamplona, along with its cardio-respiratory complications. Because of the worsening renal insufficiency, his doctors made a stricter diet plan for him and advised a lifestyle that ensured more rest. Specifically, the diet plan was low in proteins, with precise amounts of hydrates of carbon and lipids. In order not to gain weight, the diet did not include salt or an increase of liquid intake. All of these measures translated at mealtime into a first dish of vegetables that could be seasoned with a little oil, either without salt or with non-sodium salt, and a second dish of meat or fish, strictly weighed. The dessert was almost always one fruit. He accepted the monotony of this diet, which was so tasteless, with good humor and submissive obedience to medical indications. He never asked about the specifics of his sickness, and when, on occasion, it seemed advisable for him to know them so that he could comply fully with the directives, he showed absolute trust in the doctors, accepting whatever Msgr. Álvaro and Msgr. Javier told to him to do, as prescribed by the doctors. Msgr. Javier gave the medicines that he took daily, and he never asked what they were for or what their therapeutic properties were.

"His soul pushed his body in an astonishing way"

In the medical checkups, his docility, patience, and determined effort to cooperate with the doctors were outstanding; he never showed distaste for the discomforts that every medical examination entailed. He was very open to all questions, letting himself be examined from head to toe with an indulgent and submissive attitude as the doctors moved him, raised him, extracted blood from him, and took his radiography and electrocardiogram. At the same time, he would not let himself be served. It was difficult to help him take off his clothes, to unbutton and remove the cufflinks of his shirt because, with quick and animated movements, he would anticipate those of his medical examiners. Whenever they succeeded in unbuttoning his shirt, he would take their hands and kiss them.

He was usually full of praise, affection, and gratitude toward those who looked after his health. His usual generosity led him to send gifts as tokens of his gratitude. As a concrete example, in April 1972 in Madrid, he gave Professor Ortiz de Landázuri a wooden cross, something close to his heart and which hung in his room, as a spontaneous gesture of his generous spirit.

To the doctor's question about the state of his health, his usual response was that he found himself well. "I am fine," he used to say, but then he would turn to Msgr. Álvaro and Msgr. Javier and add, "but they can tell you what they think."

Two months of priestly activity that he undertook in October and November 1972 throughout Spain and Portugal stand out in the two years of St. Josemaría's life from 1972 to 1974. After his medical checkup in the University Hospital, he started those two months of very intense preaching in Pamplona, Bilbao, Madrid, Oporto, Lisboa, Sevilla, Valencia, and Barcelona. On November 30, he returned to Rome.

In that medical examination, as in other previous ones, his doctors urged St. Josemaría to have a daily stroll, to rest after lunch and, if possible, to keep his day free from anxieties and excessive work. Ordinarily, he would make himself available for anyone or any work that needed his presence, not observing the medical advice given especially in regard to the after-meal rest, the *siesta;* he never took it, for ascetical reasons and also because he did not have a free minute; he could not nor did he want to flee from the contradictions of each day because he was very firm and clear about serving others for the love of God. When his doctors advised him to consider going out of Rome for a change of air so that while he was pushing the apostolic undertaking he could rest, his answer would be something like this: *"I have to be in Rome; it is my cross and I cannot but embrace it."*

St. Josemaría found that time of catechesis to be ideal for him in spite of the exhausting work that he carried out: every day he spoke to veritable multitudes in get-togethers that lasted a long time. Moreover, he daily received many people in small groups, at the same time participating in different liturgical ceremonies, which undoubtedly made him tired. Those who knew the intensity of his priestly work commented about it, astonished, and the physicians who knew about his delicate health could not find any satisfactory explanation without recourse to affirming that his love and zeal for souls were what sustained and provided him with such intense vigor, which is unusual even in persons healthier and younger than the Founder.

At this time one of St. Josemaría's old symptoms acquired greater importance: the nocturnal insomnia, which could be explained as a result of the elevated uremia and the accentuated anemia. However, the ultimate explanation could undoubtedly be found in the time of crisis within the Church—which had already been denounced by Pope Paul VI and which made him lose sleep when he would remain many hours, at times entire nights, in a vigil of prayer. He used to repeat to the people who lived with him, *"I suffer for the Church."* The doctors were aware of this situation through the information provided by Msgr. Álvaro and Msgr. Javier. In order to combat his insomnia, the doctors changed the type of sleeping pill he took; but they were not successful in solving the situation, and he suffered from insomnia until the end of his life.

The central event of the period between May and September 1974 was St. Josemaría's trip to several countries in America. Around the middle of May 1974, St. Josemaría underwent an exhaustive medical examination in Pamplona to gain advice about making this trip from the standpoint of his health.

The data analyzed showed that the renal insufficiency had continued to worsen. Despite his worsening condition, the doctors took into account the personality of St. Josemaría and advised him to go. Their experience in dealing with him had demonstrated that alterations in his physical condition, although important, did not strictly correlate with what the Founder was able to do. Some words of Msgr. Álvaro, written after the death of the saint, reflect very well the basis of the affirmative decision for the trip; in referring to the Founder, he wrote, "Immersed in God, his soul pushed his body in an astonishing way; the spiritual part predominated over the somatic part in such a way that, notwithstanding his mature age, it gave him that overflowing energy which many of you experienced during the second and third catecheses in America. Nobody can understand it any other way."[5]

In addition, the doctors greatly valued the spiritual benefit that ensued from the presence of the Founder among the faithful of Opus Dei in those nations, allowing them to hear directly from him concerning the essential aspects of the spirit of the Work. In addition, it gave St. Josemaría great spiritual joy to meet thousands of his children and to get to know about the many undertakings already operating in those countries. These were combined with his apostolic zeal and his mission to confirm souls in the faith, in love for the Church and the Pope, and in fidelity to the Magisterium.

In preparation for the journey, the doctors modified the pharmacological treatment, making yet more adjustments to the diet plan, and recommended a lifestyle that would include an apostolic activity plan less intense than on previous occasions. The fact that one of them would accompany St. Josemaría during the trip also helped his doctors arrive at an affirmative opinion.

From May 22, the date of his arrival in Brazil, up to August 31 when he returned to Europe, St. Josemaría gave himself inordinately. All throughout his itinerary in Brazil, Argentina, Chile, Peru, Ecuador, and Venezuela, he would have—when he did not have to be in bed due to serious pneumonia—several daily get-togethers, unmindful of physical tiredness and including some major illnesses, which he contracted during those more than 100 days of catechesis in America.

[5] Letter, June 29, 1975.

He adapted himself very well to the change of hemisphere, temperature, atmospheric pressure, etc. A few hours after his arrival in Brazil, he demanded pastoral work; jokingly, he said that if they would not give him much work, "I will return to Europe; I have come here to work."

The demanding schedule that he imposed on himself resulted in his being advised to take it easy, but this was not possible. Not only did he give himself generously in get-togethers attended by many people, but also met small groups and individuals, especially with the directors of Opus Dei in each country.

Thus, he spent his days in Brazil, Argentina and Chile. In Chile, some blood and urine samples were submitted to the Central Clinic Laboratory of the Catholic University of Santiago de Chile by way of a routine medical checkup. When the Chief of the Laboratory examined the results, not knowing the identity of the sick person but realizing the gravity of his sickness, he suggested that the patient remain in bed and undergo dialysis. Nevertheless, neither St. Josemaría nor those who accompanied him then learned of the medical directive in time, so in those ten days of his stay in Chile, he had 25 public gatherings with groups more or less numerous, attended separately to 13 families, visited His Holiness the Nuncio and other ecclesiastical authorities, and was, on more than 20 occasions, with the faithful of Opus Dei, in family get-togethers or in workshops. He also visited the Archbishop Cardinal of Santiago, traveled to the Shrine of Our Lady of Lo Vásquez, climbed up to greet the Virgin of Cerro, and went to the Carmel of St. Joseph, in order to have a spiritual dialogue with the Carmelite community.

His stay in Peru started with a similar rhythm of work. On July 13 he traveled from Lima to Cañete. In the evening, he showed signs of a markedly hoarse voice. Nevertheless, on July 14, he had a get-together with thousands of persons and received several families, overcoming the discomforts of what was actually an incipient bronchopulmonary complaint and the effects of an anti-infection and antihistamine medication that had been administered to him. Following doctors' advice, he stayed in bed for five days, suspending the work schedule that had been set up. After some adjustments, he complied with the new schedule until the end, preaching to thousands of people although he had not fully recuperated.

He arrived in Quito before his respiratory illness had been completely cured. The altitude of the Ecuadorian capital (he stayed in a house located almost 3,000 meters high), combined with his respiratory deficiency, resulted in his suffering from altitude sickness (what the natives called "soroche") to a significant degree, which manifested itself with nausea, vomiting, feelings of dizziness and even vertigo, deep anorexia and incapacity of movement. He would fall if there was no support, and had belabored breathing, daytime somnolence, and nocturnal insomnia.

His face showed profound tiredness. His checkup revealed an increase in the number of respirations per minute; and, at the end of his stay in Ecuador, his body manifested signs of light edema, or swelling, in the legs and ankles together with a light reactivation of pulmonary problems: slight fever, cough, and minor breathing problems. The analysis of blood and urine showed results similar to those obtained on previous occasions.

All of this could be observed medically, but the most important part of those days was the supernatural response of St. Josemaría to his difficult physical situation. His voice was weak, and he had difficulty articulating sounds. He said that he was living through days of spiritual infancy. For many years, almost 50 since his priestly ordination, he had struggled ascetically in order to make himself a child before God, and he emphasized how the Lord made him experience it in those days: weak voice, daytime somnolence, incapacity to walk without help….

No one ever saw him lose his good humor or express the least complaint for the afflictions he was suffering. His abandonment into the hands of God was absolute, although he showed his sorrow for not being able to have the previously planned apostolic get-togethers with the Ecuadorians. Above all, it pained him tremendously not to be able to celebrate the Holy Mass on those days: it was his great passion as a priest.

He joked about his illness saying, "It is because I am not a high-level person." He saw, in that situation, the loving hand of God the Father and, in spiritual conversation with those who accompanied him, he used the simile of a small child with whom his father plays. "The Lord has turned me into an infant," he would repeat frequently. At times he needed oxygen to help him breathe, and he would take the occasion to comment with good humor that he was talking to us with borrowed oxygen.

One day Dr. Azanza commented that he usually advised tourists who came to Quito and suffered from altitude sickness to abandon the capital. St. Josemaría's immediate, energetic reply was, "Yes, my son, but I am not a tourist. I am prepared to stay here for however long it takes me to get adapted, so that I can talk about God, since that's what I came here for."

Drawing strength from weakness, he had several apostolic get-togethers on August 12, 13, and 14. Some of his comments then summarize marvelously the attitude of St. Josemaría in the face of infirmity: "Jesus, I accept being conditioned these days and my whole life and whenever you want. You will give me the grace, the joy, and good humor in order to enjoy myself very much, in order to serve you, and so that the acceptance of these trifles may be a prayer full of love."

During those 15 days that he spent in Venezuela after leaving Quito, he had bronchitis with fever, and in those bad physical conditions he held several get-togethers on various occasions.

The last trip to America

Three things stood out in the period between September 1974 and February 1975:

- Notable worsening of renal insufficiency.
- Signs of cardiac insufficiency due to failure of the left ventricle brought about serious symptoms of edema of the lungs in the evening of November 10, 1974.
- A gradual loss of visual sharpness occurred in September, evidenced, first in Rome and then in Madrid, by the alteration of the retina, and above all by the beginning of opaqueness in the center of the crystal of the left eye. On the right eye there was already a condensation of crystalline fibers, with a visual sharpness only 1/3 of normal in that eye. Only those who by reason of their work were very close to the Founder knew that he could see very little: such was the naturalness with

which he endured this new complication because of his already long-experienced capacity of loving physical pain.

St. Josemaría's life during those six months was the usual one; he did not want to be exempted from his work schedule and obligations from his task of governing Opus Dei. He repeated insistently the aspirations—*Domine, ut videam! ut videamus! ut videant!*—with which he asked that the light of God illumine the consciences of those who must be lights and guides to remedy the situation of doctrinal and disciplinary confusion in so many sectors of the Church and in society.

He frequently gave thanks for the effort and affection that his daughters put into the presentation of his food, whose true content defied their external appearance. For example, what came out looking like an egg in a crust was nothing but an ingenious mixture of bread without salt and non-fat milk, or some sweet dessert without sugar or egg yolk which the kitchen attendants made using substitutes.

During his stay in those two American countries, St. Josemaría strictly fulfilled the doctors' indications. But what the doctors could not control was the apostolic zeal and love of God in his heart which led him to talk the whole day about God under any circumstances.

The Founder seemed to experience a perfect harmony between what is psychosomatic and what is supernatural: he could quickly shift from a condition of profound tiredness to one lively activity when he would talk about God. Literally rising from his sickbed, he would show great vitality in preaching and make his listeners vibrate with him. In those weeks of stay in Venezuela and Guatemala he would get up, despite his fever, from his bed to go to his appointments. At the end of the activity, he would find himself exhausted, and later advised again to take a rest so he may recover.

The last months

He spent the months between February 27 and May 18 of 1975 in Rome. Medical data showed that he continued to suffer from renal insufficiency; his anemia worsened, and his cholesterol level shot up. The cardiac insufficiency persisted; he experienced swelling in his legs, and it became difficult to regulate the equilibrium of fluids in his body. During the first days of May, he experienced an episode of cardiac asthma, a foreshadow of what was to come later in May. Observers would have found little correlation between these distressful health conditions and his active normal work schedule.

Between May 15 and June 26, 1975, the renal insufficiency seemed to stabilize, but the cardiac problems became worrisome. The first cardiac asthma crisis on May 3 was followed by two more incidents in that month: a severe edema of the lungs on the evening of the 21st until the next day and another cardiac asthma crisis on May 30th.

St. Josemaría spent May 23 to 26 in Torreciudad because the city of Barbastro wanted to award him with a Gold Medal. Though he refused to receive the award, he later acceded to give a push to this apostolic undertaking. He took advantage of this trip to Torreciudad to pray to the Virgin at the Shrine, whose construction was practically finished. He went through the various locations while overcoming his usual tiredness.

The trip to Torreciudad started exactly two days after the second cardiac incident in May. Then, on the 24th, he learned of the death of Don Salvador Canals.[6] His grief and the lingering effects of the cardiac crisis manifested itself the following day in the ceremony when the City Council of Barbastro presented him with the Gold Medal of the city. His voice cracked from emotion and exhaustion as he remembered his deceased son.

On his return to Madrid, he went to consult Dr. Ulpiano Arias for a complete dental prosthesis. On May 31, moments before leaving for Rome, he commented in a confidential tone about how sorry he was for the inconveniences he had caused the doctors during that visit.

He said that when he was younger, it never crossed his mind that the Lord was going to put him in that situation. "Now," he added, "I ask him to take me whenever he wants, without giving any trouble; here, I am nothing but a bother. From heaven I will be able to help you more and better."[7]

Less than a month later, the Lord granted his desire.

[6] Salvador Canals was one of the oldest priests of the Prelature. He arrived in Rome in 1942 to study Canon Law, and there he lived the rest of his life (he received priestly ordination in 1948). He carried out an intense pastoral work at the service of the Church. He was a member of the Tribunal of the Roman Rota and a consultant to the diverse dicasteries of the Holy See.

[7] Editor's Note: Cfr. Álvaro del Portillo, *The Founder of Opus Dei*, Scepter Publishers, New York 2005, pp. 231-252. Vázquez de Prada. A., *o.c.*, III, p. 680.

Chapter 3

Pain as Taught by St. Josemaría*

> Don't complain if you suffer. It is the prized and valued stone that is polished.
>
> Does it hurt? Allow yourself to be cut gratefully, because God has taken you in his hands as if you were a diamond. An ordinary pebble is not worked on like that.
>
> Furrow, 235

Identification with Christ

Perhaps the Founder of Opus Dei founded his vision of the sick on a point of *The Way*. It says: "Children...the sick...As you write these words, don't you feel tempted to write them with capitals? The reason is that in little children and in the sick a soul in love sees him!"[1]

From these words emanate the whole of his attitude toward the sick, in whom he saw a concentration of pain and whom he beheld as gifted with a greater density of God.

What can we expect of someone in love with God and who considers the sick as God, carrying his most intimate convictions to the end? Very simply, St. Josemaría felt for the sick a love as infinite as the sea.

* This article was written by Jesus Honorato, Director of Pharmacological Services of the University Hospital.

[1] Cfr. *The Way*, no. 419.

This identification with Christ appears numerous times in his writings, homilies, and get-togethers with that expression of his, so much on fire and eager to ask that the light of God may shine.

In November 1972, while closing a large get-together in Barcelona, St Josemaría said, "A sick person awaits me, and I do not have the right to make a sick person wait, who is Christ." He was capable of sacrificing anything, no matter how much he liked it (and get-togethers with his children were something he liked most), in order to be close to a sick person because he considered that person to be full of Him.

On one occasion in addressing himself to a professor in a school of nurses, our first Chancellor told her, "I love nurses in a very special way. In the middle of the world, you are extraordinary. You know how to smile even when you are already tired and bothered. You know how to conduct yourselves with the kindness of a mother with people who are strangers to you. God bless you! Imagine that you are serving the family of Nazareth, that that sick person is Christ."

Here again the key idea is identification of the sick with Christ, and from it he deduced, with relentless logic, his admiration and affection for a profession which, aside from being sacrificing, affords the priceless opportunity of being close to Him and being able to show Him direct kindness and affection.

Many other quotations could be presented that have a direct and profound bearing on this identification. The idea that where there is pain there is Christ, permanently dominates the undertaking of St. Josemaría like those glittering rocks at dusk that reflect a sun that never sets.

His love for the sick was like a river that never ceases to flow.

Sickness is a source of virtue, strength and grace

Since the sick are Christ, and Christ is the source of all grace and strength, it is necessary to love the patient so that we may receive grace and strength. It is not surprising, therefore, that when St. Josemaría found himself called to begin Opus Dei, he realized the enormous effort it would take, and he understood that he had no other recourse than to respond. He sought to gain fortitude by approaching the sick in the hospitals of Madrid, first in the *Patronato de Enfermos* (Patronage for the Sick) and afterwards in the provincial hospitals, where he carried out an immense work of charity and apostolate in the 1920s and the first years of the 1930s. He liked to recall that "the human strength of the Work has been the sick of the hospitals of Madrid: the most miserable ones; those who lived in their houses, hanging on to the last human hope; the most ignorant of those very poor slum dwellers. These are the ambitions of Opus Dei, the human means that we used: the incurable sick, the abandoned poor, uncultured children without family, homes without fire, warmth and love."[2]

Not only do those assisting the sick thereby seek grace, but also the patient himself must make good use of his situation in order to grow in stature and become close to God: "When you are ill, offer up your sufferings with love, and they will turn into incense rising up in God's honor, and making you holy,"[3] St. Josemaría said. "Pain, make

[2] Cfr. Sastre, A., *Tiempo de caminar,* Rialp, Madrid, 1991. p. 113.
[3] *The Forge,* no. 791.

good use of it!"[4] Those who flee like a coward from suffering have something to meditate upon when they see the enthusiasm with which other souls embrace pain. "There are many men and women who know how to suffer in a Christian way. Let us follow their example."[5] And in another place, he wrote, "Thank him for everything, because everything is good."[6]

It would be well to note that our Founder did not seek illness as a motive of mortification; rather, with a grand simplicity, he made good use of it. "Physical pain, when it can be removed, it is removed. There are enough sufferings in life! And when it cannot be removed, it is offered."[7] He always had the precise word, the secret of rightly employing exactly the right concept.

We should never waste time, and so, although sickness may mean a period of inactivity, we have to exploit it, an idea that he expresses through a very beautiful image: "The plants were hidden under the snow. And the farmer, the owner of the land, remarked with satisfaction: 'Now they're growing on the inside.' I thought of you, of your forced inactivity... Tell me, are you also growing on the inside?"[8]

Similarly, sickness can be used as an exercise of humility and trust in God. When María Ignacia García Escobar, a young woman admitted to the King's Hospital with an incurable tuberculosis, saw that her death was approaching, she heard St. Josemaría say the following: "Sometimes it can appear to us that God is hard on us; we cannot under-

[4] Cfr. Sastre, A., *o.c.*, p. 118.
[5] *Furrow*, no. 236.
[6] Cfr. *The Way*, no. 268.
[7] Cfr. *En memoria...*, *o.c.*, p. 153
[8] *The Way*, no. 294.

stand the difficulties and pains that he sends us; but neither does a small child understand why his mother doesn't let him play with a knife or to touch the candle's flame with his fingers; even less does he understand, under specific circumstances, why he receives a spanking. However, everything is for the good."[9] It is difficult to express in a few words the saint's whole treatise of humility, resignation, love of God, completed with the note of optimism and joy so characteristic of his manner of being.

Joy was another immense facet of his life; illness is applicable not only to obtain grace and fortitude and many other virtues, but also it is a source of joy, and St. Josemaría explained it very well when he said, "You suffer in this present life, which is only a dream, and a short one at that. Rejoice, because your Father God loves you so much, and if you put no obstacles in his way, after this bad dream he will give you a good awakening."[10]

These few quotations demonstrate well the idea that our Founder had of sickness as a spring of virtues, as something which, although it can appear like suffering, is not only tremendously productive, but also can even be and must be converted into a source of joy. When one has been treating the sick for quite some time, one comes to understand that it is practically impossible to give them greater consolation and therefore better medicine than providing them with this very positive vision of the so-called morbid process, which is converted thus into a process of grandeur that brings them close to God.

[9] Cfr. Sastre, A., *Tiempo de caminar, o.c.*, p. 114.
[10] *The Way*, no. 692.

Sickness is a privilege

If the sick person identifies himself with Christ and if sickness is a spring of goodness and energy, the conclusion is very clear: sickness is a privilege. St. Josemaría liked to say, frequently and simply, "The sick, they are the favorite of God."[11]

During his work in the Provincial Hospital of Madrid, St. Josemaría continuously asked for the prayers of the sick for matters with particular urgency, and he told them: "Do not forget that the sick are very pleasing to God, and that their prayer is heard and rises to the presence of the Lord."[12] In a trip through South America, in San Paulo he commented, "The sick are children of God and very much loved by him: they have more opportunities than anyone to offer the Lord a thousand things, to smile...How difficult it is for a sick person to smile!"[13] In *The Way*, St. Josemaría wrote, "After the prayer of priests and of consecrated virgins, the prayer most pleasing to God is that of children and of the sick."[14] St. Josemaría had arrived at this affirmation after a process of reflection in which he saw that because illness is such an enormous privilege that it cannot be quantified, then the prayer of the sick must be valuable indeed. In a get-together held in Buenos Aires in 1974, he addressed a woman who gave thanks to the Work for the help she had received for her husband who had just died, and the Father told her, "And you have my prayer which, for being the prayer of a priest, is worth something: almost as much as that of a sick person."[15]

[11] Cfr. *En memoria..., o.c.,* p.138.
[12] Cfr. Sastre, A., *Tiempo de caminar, o.c.,* p. 111.
[13] Cfr. *En memoria... o.c.,* p. 142.
[14] Cfr. *The Way,* no. 98.
[15] Cfr. *En memoria... o.c.,* p. 167.

In any case, he considered the sick to be so privileged that it aroused in him holy envy. On one occasion, in addressing a cardiologist who commented to him how difficult it was to become accustomed to the sight of pain and death, St. Josemaría told him, referring to himself and to his early times of work in the hospitals of Madrid, "I liked very much to visit the sick poor people, and once I found myself as in many other similar situations at the deathbed of a dying young man. It pained me to see him die, but at that moment I envied him. I saw that that soul was going straight, purified, to the Lord and I told him: 'I envy you!' He died consoled, very happy."[16] With a simple and transparent example like this, he could demonstrate at the same time pain and consolation, generosity and envy, and pain and love all direct toward Christ. His generosity, his obstinate love, his invincible truth, his faithful light helped him to discern joy in everything and to find joy in everyone.

In order to round off his concept of sickness as a privilege, as something that "distinguishes" the soul before God, we can quote a passage from *Furrow*: "Don't complain if you suffer. It is the prized and valued stone that is polished. Does it hurt? Allow yourself to be cut, gratefully, because God has taken you in his hands as if you were a diamond. An ordinary pebble is not worked on like that."[17]

We can see that the vision of St. Josemaría transcended a mere physical plane and was founded concretely on the most pure love for Christ, because He and the sick are one. Being sick signifies that one is a favorite of God, and if strength and grace are obtained from Christ, one has to get close to the patient, console him, and help him—because also in this way, and perhaps thus in a more direct way,

[16] Cfr. *En memoria... o.c.*, p. 167.
[17] *Furrow*, no. 235.

sanctification is attained. St. Josemaría knew how to bring this theory into practice; and when he started working with the sick, nobody like him had brought the celestial influence of love to places bereft of joy, like the hospitals of Madrid, where dawn found it more difficult than in any other place to overcome the night.

Exaltation of life

A person's understanding of life is innate to his way of looking at death. In St. Josemaría the profound respect that he felt for life as something not our own, powerfully commanded attention. He knew that life is from God and that death was, therefore, diminished in importance.

One would say that death bothered him only because it impedes working for Christ here on earth where many things have to be done; otherwise, death is but a biological phenomenon with hardly any transcendence; it is simply a change of life. Many times he would say, "without fear of life, and without fear of death."[18] He saw death as a bird in flight, as a murmur of the golden leaves that smoothly pass through their brief existence.

Some of the most beautiful words uttered about life St. Josemaría delivered on the occasion of the investiture of Professor Lejeune as Doctor *honoris causa* at the University of Navarre. On that occasion he said, "Human lives, which are holy, come from God; they cannot be treated like simple things, like numbers of statistics. Upon considering the profound reality of life, its most noble affections escape from the human heart."[19] Going deeper along the same

[18] Cfr. *En memoria... o.c.*, p. 173.

[19] The commitment of truth, May 9, 1974. *Josemaría Escrivá and the University*, EUNSA, Pamplona 1993, p. 108.

lines, he tells us in *The Way*: "If you lose the supernatural meaning of your life, your charity will be philanthropy; your purity, decency; your mortification, stupidity; your discipline, a lash; and all your works, fruitless."[20]

Applying the same supernatural vision of life as something that does not belong to us when speaking about death, he expresses himself in this sense: "God is the owner of life and death. God does not act like a hunter. The Lord is like a gardener; when He sees that a soul is ready He brings him to Heaven."[21] It becomes absolutely clear that life is not ours; it has a supernatural projection because it is a patrimony of God; therefore, He is the only one who has the right over it, especially at the moment that He considers opportune. If a person loses this supernatural meaning, he is useless. That is why the actions of those who work against life, both in its beginning as well as in its end, hurt the saint in his soul.

He expressed in a categorical way his rejection of all attempts to do away with the life of others. His rejection of abortion was so profound, so radical, and so vivid that he did not even mention the word. In his way of understanding life as something that comes from God, abortion was something so repugnant that he could not understand that such a word exists to define a situation so outrageous. Likewise, any idea of euthanasia was rejected. The Church, taking as her example the sufferings of Christ, has always considered the justifications of those who advocate euthanasia as false compassion. In *The Forge*, he said: "To die is a good thing. How can anyone with faith, at the same time, be afraid to die? But as long as the Lord wants to keep you

[20] *The Way*, no. 280

[21] Recorded by Msgr. Álvaro del Portillo in a get-together in IPADE, Mexico, May 8, 1983.

here on earth, it would be cowardice for you to want to die. You must live and suffer and work for Love: that is your task."[22]

Concerning death, the only pejorative aspect it had on him is that it interrupts a work of service to God, because life also must be understood as a constant and productive dedication to the glory to God. On another occasion, he wrote: "Some give too much importance to age, when they are still very young. Only those years we spend serving God really count."[23]

Neither did he like wasting the time that life itself gives. "How little a life is to offer to God!...."[24]

"The life of man upon earth is a warfare." So said Job many centuries ago. There are still some easygoing individuals unaware of this fact."[25]

But it is not only a question of making good use of life, generally speaking. It is also a matter of making good use of it minute by minute and second by second; hence our Founder insisted, "Every instant has the meaning of eternity. This world, my children, is slipping from our hands. We cannot waste time, which is short: it is necessary that we strive in our task of personal sanctification and apostolic work, which the Lord has entrusted to us: we have to spend time faithfully, loyally, administering well with a sense of responsibility the talents we have received."[26] It would be difficult to find more beautiful words, phras-

[22] *The Forge,* no. 1037.

[23] Get-together in Villa Tevere, Rome, January 9, 1974.

[24] *The Way,* no. 420.

[25] *Ibid.,* no. 306.

[26] Editor's Note. Cfr. Informative Bulletin of Josemaría Escrivá; no. 1, May 1976, p. 4.

es with more meaning, that could serve as an end to the theme at hand.

Our Founder was himself a university who helped people understand sickness and taught them to love life, a university who knew how to solve the shadow in science and the sickness in strength and life with the certainty and power of the bright stars that shine for God.

Addressing doctors and nurses

The foregoing ideas also appear in various words that the Founder of the Work addressed to doctors and nurses. They are expressions of gratitude for the work that such professionals carry out in service to people. They are also voices of encouragement that push them not to abandon the constant task of improvement in professional formation, in order to serve better. They are appeals to the sense of responsibility as Christians, with respect to the spiritual assistance that should be given to the sick.

As a priest, he saw the health professions as analogous to the priesthood because they constitute an active and zealous submission to a service full of nobility to people; hence his words are spoken as from a priest of Jesus Christ. He explained it when he was asked by a stress doctor how he could avoid routine and lukewarmness in his professional work. The Founder of Opus Dei answered him: "Have presence of God, as you are already doing. Yesterday I was with a sick person, someone whom I love with all my heart as Father, and I understand the great priestly work that you doctors do. But do not become proud, because all souls are priestly. One has to activate that priesthood! When you wash your hands, when you put on the surgical robe, when you wear the gloves, think of God, and think of that royal priesthood of which St. Peter speaks; and you then will not be tepid: you will do good to bodies and souls."

A year and a half later, in a get-together that many of us will remember always—it was the last time that our first Chancellor was at the University of Navarre—a nurse of the University Hospital asked him how she could improve in her work. Enjoying the opportunity that was being offered to him to reiterate counsels and expectations which he had expressed on other instances, he answered:

> Nurses from many nations, many times, have asked me this question. I am happy that you are asking me this or similar questions, because it is necessary to have many Christian nurses since your work is a priesthood, as much as and more than that of doctors. I was going to say more, because you have the finesse—pardon me, the courtesy—the *immediacy*, because you are always beside the sick persons. The doctor comes, and then leaves; he will keep them in mind, but he does not have them constantly in front of him. That is why I think that to be a nurse is a special vocation of a Christian. But in order for that vocation to be perfected, it is necessary for you nurses to be very well prepared scientifically, and also that you are very kind: to have that finesse that the School and the University Clinic of Navarre is known for. May God bless you, my daughter!

He also expected these two attributes of finesse and scientific knowledge from doctors:

> I am moved...when they tell me about something that many of you must have experienced. Doctors cannot help but act like confessors, but in what is material: and the doctors here are not only concerned about the body, but also the soul. They have the same concern as you, and they don't say to someone: "take off your clothes," just like that... Everybody comments to me the same thing: what finesse (*delicadeza*)! What attention! One can see that they know their science; but, above all, aside from being great men and great doctors, they have an extraordinary finesse.
>
> Now, doctors should not become proud because others do the same, each one in his own field. Emulation, it is good that there be, so that each day you will be more tactful, more Christian; not only wiser, not only more masterful, but also more of a disciple of Christ.

These words, uttered in the very last get-together of St. Josemaría at the University of Navarre, have the value of a testament, of a last will, that all of us working in this University have to strive to fulfill.

For the nurse, the doctor, being a disciple of Christ is concretized in details, of which we can enumerate only a few: love for the Sacraments, a profound understanding of death, a solid meaning of the value of life.

Our first Chancellor said the following to a doctor in Peru—in reply to a question about how to overcome the intense fear of death shown by the sick and their relatives and even by the doctors—about how to succeed in considering death like a "good friend":

> Listen, my son, I am going to tell you a short anecdote. Not long ago, a friend of yours, whom perhaps you know personally—he is a man who manages companies, he is very busy, and he travels constantly from one place to another—was explaining to me that he regularly meets with other colleagues and makes a quarterly or bimonthly plan of work: it's wonderful... because they cover all possibilities, all, all! Except one, and I tell them: "You, who have foreseen this, that or the other, have you considered that we can die...?" Tremendous! They have not considered it, and it is the only sure thing. The only sure thing!
>
> Death, my children, is not an unpleasant passage. Death is a door that open us to Love, to Love in capital letters, to happiness, to rest, to joy. One should not wait for it with fear. It is true that a doctor considers it from other points of view; but a Christian doctor, like you—you made me realize how you see it, may God bless you!—must look at it in a positive way. And the others as well. It is not the end, it is the beginning. For a Christian, to die is not to die; it is to live. To live in capital letters. And so, do not be afraid of death.
>
> Confront death. Face it. Count on it; it has to come... Why are you going to be afraid? To hide the head under the wing with fear, with panic, why? Lord,

> life is death. Lord, death for a Christian is rest, it is Love, and from there I don't go out. Was this what you wanted me to tell you?

For the nurses, he was never lacking, aside from words of affection, in words to remind them of the dignity of their profession and the collaboration that they can always give to the fulfillment of the redemptive plan of God, helping in so many instances the sick to receive spiritual help and the Sacraments. On one occasion he said to a professor in the School of Nurses:

> I love, in a special way, the nurses. In the middle of the world, I see you as something extraordinary. You know how to smile when you are already tired and troubled. You know how to have the affection of a mother towards people who really are strangers to you.
>
> May God bless you. Think that you are serving the family of Nazareth, that that sick person is Christ. He has said it, remember? Or that she is the Mother of God. Bring them to me with affection, with care, with kindness. Nothing should be lacking to them; above all, spiritual help. Prepare them well. May God bless you! I bless all the nurses everywhere.

And he added on another occasion, words very similar to what I have just transcribed: … "I pray for you, because I think of the good and the evil that you can do. When a person is prepared, he can be told even brusquely, without any problem, the truth about his condition. If a person is not ready, make good use of every opportunity so that he can confess and receive Communion, and so that he goes to Communion again. And the moment comes when these very sick children will want to be told that they are going to heaven. I know of very beautiful cases."

How many times did the Founder of Opus Dei recommend feeding personal prayer with the happenings of the day, "up to the smallest details of the day"[27] because God is "a loving spectator of our entire day."[28] And it is in prayer where we manage to give meaning to things that we do not understand. There are doctors and nurses who never get used to death. A Brazilian doctor confided to St. Josemaría that, in spite of his daily contact with sickness and having a Christian outlook, he would always experience the impact of death and sorrow, especially in young people. The Father showed him how those sentiments have to be completed and purified with acts of faith, with prayer:

> I am going to tell you an anecdote, my son. There was a young priest who had to fulfill a mission…a world mission. He didn't have virtues, and neither does he have them now: almost fifty years have passed, forty-seven… He didn't have virtues or money. He only had youth, good humor, and the grace of God. He liked very much to visit the sick poor people, and once he found himself, as in many similar instances before, at the deathbed of a pitiful dying young man. Situations like this saddened me, but at that moment I envied him. I saw that that soul was going straight, purified, to the Lord and I

[27] Life of prayer (homily delivered on April 4, 1955), in *Friends of God, o.c,* n. 246.

[28] *Ibid,* no. 245.

told him: "I envy you!" He departed very consoled, very happy.

Perhaps you, sometimes, will feel somewhat envious of those dying persons and at other times feeling sad because they lacked Christian resignation. Pray for them. Be a good doctor, as you already are; a good Christian, as you are; and you will do great work.

I want to close this part with those words that St. Josemaría addressed to the doctors, words that as Chancellor he uttered at the University of Navarre, during the solemn investiture of an honorary doctorate. He said:

> The University of Navarre owes a lot to Professor Jiménez Díaz, and it is for me a great joy to have the opportunity to acknowledge it once more. From the very outset, he understood the transcendence of this educative and scientific undertaking, and with his experience and encouragement, he collaborated effectively to make it a reality. He was the first President of the Association of Friends of the University of Navarre, and until his death he had been Honorary President. The Doctorate *honoris causa* that today is conferred on him posthumously, and the stone plaque that will honor his memory in the School of Medicine, are the homage of admiration and gratitude to the illustrious scientist, honorable man, a very dear friend.[29]

[29] Josemaría Escrivá and the University, EUNSA, Pamplona 1993, p. 93.

One more thing hould be noted: how strong was St. Josemaría's sense of friendship, how strong his fidelity, how firm his gratitude!

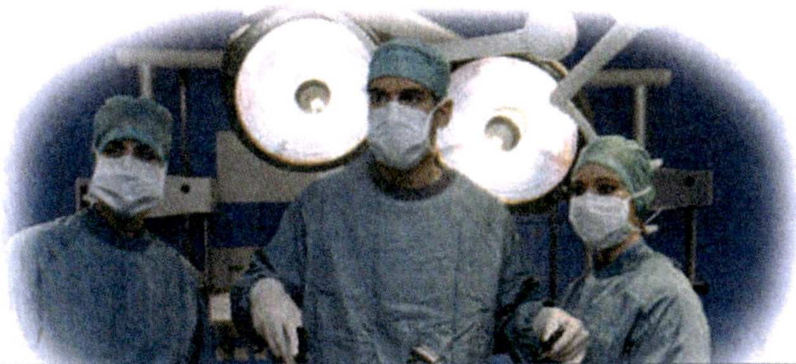

Chapter 4

Testimonies of Doctors who have Known and Personally Dealt with St Josemaría*

> "Children. The sick. As you write these words, don't you feel tempted to write them with capitals? The reason is that in little children and in the sick a soul in love sees him!"
>
> *The Way*, n. 419

"Without Fear of Life and Without Fear of Death"

The identification of the sick with Christ serves as the foundation of all that St Josemaría had lived and taught in relation to medicine. It is an identification that has enkindled a love for those who suffer in so many souls for over two thousand years, as you well know.

The Founder would point out that the sick are God's favorites and also the treasure of the Work. He earnestly

*This chapter gathers a collection of interesting testimonies of Spanish doctors who have either known or dealt personally with St Josemaría and were involved during the early years of the University Clinic and the University of Navarre.

Among these were **Dr. Gonzalo Herranz**, a world authority in bioethics and deontology and **Dr. Manuel Nevado,** whose inexplicable cure prompted the process of canonization of Blessed Josemaría.

Their testimonies were modified for purposes of brevity and their relevance to the topics dealt with in this book.

sought their prayers which are very powerful in the eyes of God. He considered the sicknesses he endured between 1940 and 1950 as signs of divine predilection.

During one of his catechetical trips throughout the Iberian peninsula and South America, someone asked him: "Father…I would like you to explain to us what you mean when you say that the treasure of Opus Dei is the sick?" The Father answered:

> Listen, my son, there was a priest… Do we go further? there was a boy who began to love, and that he felt the certainty that God wanted something from him, and he did not know what it was. Because he had no intention of becoming a priest, he told himself: perhaps in this way, I will get to know what God wants, and so he consulted, first his parents, and then his father, whom he had neither seen cry before nor after, told him, as two tears came to his eyes: "I will not object, but think about it." *I have thought a lot about it.* "Well, then go ahead. I will introduce you to a friend who can give you some guidance." And so, he did. And that priest—26 years of age, with the grace of God and good humor and nothing more—afterwards had to do Opus Dei… And do you know how he managed? Through the hospitals. That General Hospital of Madrid full of sick people, very poor, with some lying on the corridors because there were no beds; that hospital, the King's Hospital it was called, where the sick were suffering from advanced tuberculosis, and during that time tuberculosis could not be cured—now it can be cured; doctors have made a lot of progress. These were the weapons used to conquer! This was the treasure to pay off! That gave the strength to go forward!...And the Lord led us everywhere and so we are in Europe,

in Asia, in Africa, in America and in Oceania, thanks to the sick who are a treasure. I will not forget that poor creature whom I, a young priest, was helping at her deathbed after giving her Extreme Unction, and whispering into her ears: "Blessed be pain!"—that is liberation—; "loved be pain!", and she was repeating it with a broken voice: and she died in just a few minutes. "Sanctified be pain! Glorified be pain!" And I have not changed my mind. I was madly envious of her."[1]

"That woman had had a great economic and social position in life, and she was there, on a hard-old bed in a hospital, dying and alone, without anyone except me to keep her company at that moment, until she died. And she was repeating, relishing, happy: 'Blessed be pain!'—she was suffering from all moral and physical pains— "beloved be pain, sanctified be pain, glorified be pain!" Suffering is a proof that one knows how to love, that one has a heart."

This moving testimony may be completed with some words said by the Founder in an intimate get-together with a small group of his sons. It was March 19, 1975, the last feast of St. Joseph that he celebrated here on earth. There were only a few days left before the golden anniversary of his ordination. Perhaps the occasion stirred up memories of his first years as priest and Founder. He started saying:

> I was looking for strength in the poorest barrios of Madrid. For hours and hours in all places, everyday on foot, among the embarrassing and miserable poor, who had absolutely nothing; among children with runny noses, dirty, but children who wanted to please God.

[1] Editor's Note: Get-together in Tabancura, Santiago de Chile, July 2, 1974: cfr. Bernal, S., *Profile of Msgr. Escrivá, Founder of Opus Dei*, pp. 189-190; Vásquez de Prada, A., o.c. I, p. 443.

What indignation my priestly soul feels when they say that now children should not go to confession while they are still small! It is not true! They must go to personal, auricular, and secret confession, like the others. And how good it is, what a joy! I spent many hours in that task, but I regret that there could have been more. In the hospitals, and in homes where there were sick people, if they can even be called homes...They were abandoned and sick; some with tuberculosis, an incurable disease then.

It was through these means that I sought to do the Work of God, in all those places...

They were intense years when Opus Dei was growing from within without our realizing it. But I wanted to tell you that the human strength of the Work was the sick in the hospitals of Madrid: the most miserable ones; those who lived in their homes and who had lost all human hope; the most ignorant of the poorest slum areas...

These are the aspirations of Opus Dei, the human means that we applied: incurable sick, abandoned poor, kids without family and culture, homes without fire, warmth and love.[2]

His personal experience of pain

St. Josemaría could justly say that he himself knew a little of that divine subject of pain. I would like to cite here two traits. The first is the inseparable character that pain and sorrow had in his life. *"In laetitia, nulla dies sine Cruce" (With joy, no day without the Cross)* he wrote frequently in his *Epacta*,[3] indicating an aspiration for the year about to

[2] Bernal S. o.c., pp. 188-89; AA. VV., *Msgr. Josemaría Escrivá and Opus Dei. On its 50th anniversary foundation*, 2a ed., EUNSA, Pamplona 1985, pp. 24-25.

[3] Editor's Note. The *Epacta* is a liturgical calendar for assigning

begin and, at the same time, recalling an experience that was repeated every year. That deep joy that was ardently achieved with his smiling asceticism, the result of his constant searching for God.

On one occasion in Sao Paulo, he said that being sick is not a limitation for doing apostolate:

> "Father, I am sick...*Por eso!* The sick are God's beloved children: they have more opportunities than anyone else to offer a thousand things to God. A smile...how difficult it is for a sick person to smile! I knew a poor man, a sinner, who had diabetes for 10 years. He was very sick; he was dying slowly. When he smiled, and he was almost always smiling, it cost him a lot, but you must smile. You have to make life pleasant for the others. Even with that, you will attract souls.

His extensive experiences with the sick produced so many details full of humaneness! I find especially charming the words he used to address those who suffered the afflictions that he himself had experienced. On one occasion, he saw a son of his looking serious because he had facial paralysis *(a frigore)*. St Josemaría showed his affection with a touch of humor:

> "My son, don't look too serious...! I also had a face like that some 20 years ago. There were three who witnessed this in Rome, but it was not a weather joke: it was because we had no heating, and there was horrible humidity. Don't worry, you will get well. Go and see a doctor, and the problem will be solved with electricity. You will be more handsome than you were before."

the Prayers appropriate for each day, both in the eucharistic celebration as well as in the Liturgy of the Hours.

Those who had diabetes received a special show of affection:

> *"De modo que- anímate!* You are going through things I have gone through. And I am a poor man. In a way that you can, you will be able to bear those contradictions—that small cross with so much joy, when our Lord carried for us a much bigger Cross."

There was nothing artificial in his preaching. His teachings on the supernatural value of sickness are profoundly empirical, a result previously lived and experienced. He immediately connected Gospel doctrine with the ordinary life of a Christian. His manner of narrating in the third person manifests his desire to disappear and to pass unnoticed. Whenever he mentioned his own pains, it was to cheer up the afflicted with consoling words and to give them a positive outlook.

He gave this advice to parents who had sick children:

> I will tell you the experience of someone who was for ten years with a serious illness without cure. He was always happy because he abandoned himself in the arms of God, convinced that God is not an *entelequia,* a distant & far-away being. God is more than a good mother. I repeat what I said before; He is all-powerful. He does not rejoice in our misfortunes. When you remove a knife, a razor or some matchsticks from the hands of your child, he will complain because you are taking away his toy. You remove it because you are afraid the child may hurt himself. We view this world as seen from the back of a tapestry where the knots are. We do not realize that happiness comes later, and this will go away as easily as water passes through our hands. This life is fleeting. *Tempus breve est,* the Holy

Spirit affirms. There is very little time to love. Tell them about me, from someone who was sick, slowly dying; even more—that he died, but he lives out there, still moving about. Insistently tell them that the Lord of Heaven is their Father and the time to love is short. Let them fall in love here! And may that love be manifested in pain. There is an old poem ... will you excuse me for being corny? The poem is very bad, but the idea is good:

My life is wholly of love
and if in love I am well-versed
It is because of the power of pain;
for there is no better lover
than he who has shed many tears.

And men also cry. But allow them to wipe away their tears. Because what God is doing is to show them His predilection. So much joy awaits them! So much happiness awaits them forever. Tell them!

That self-surrender to the divine will was shown also in the way he faithfully complied with the doctors' prescriptions. He provoked laughter when he commented on the need to speak trustingly in spiritual direction and to practice savage sincerity. He would refer to the parallel situation of a sick person being examined by the doctor.

What are doctors for? Why do we tell them things which happen to us? I have a little pharyngitis, which is nothing... I called the doctor, a brother of yours, and he told me, "Open your mouth." I opened my mouth. He came with a small flashlight, and he pressed my tongue down.... I let him do everything he wanted to. He reached in farther, but he did not find my tonsils

> because I had them removed many years ago. It didn't embarrass me. Why should it embarrass me? Well, if I want to be cured in the soul…I must do the same thing with my body…. You tell them what you feel; they ask you questions and you allow them to examine you, that is, you let them put the light inside and you allow them to give you medicine…and every three hours you will take these. But the doctor didn't trust me. He gave them to Msgr. Javier, who will come and give me pills I have to take every three hours. I did not close my mouth: I would swallow the pill. Now I tell you, I will do whatever they tell me.

There was only one occasion when he did not exactly comply with medical instructions. It was in 1946 when he was very sick. He himself described his condition with these words:

> When I went to bed at night, I didn't know if I would get up the following day, and when I got up I didn't know if I would go back to bed…I can die even today: this can happen to any one of us. But being seriously sick as I was then…I had never been happier than in those ten years!"

Added to these physical sufferings was the responsibility to open the juridical solution for the Work, to look for a place for Opus Dei in ecclesiastical law. This demand was urged by the dedication of thousands of souls to God in his Work; nevertheless, the difficulties blocking the way to reach an appropriate solution seemed insurmountable. Thus it became necessary for the Founder to be in Rome, disregarding the advice of the doctor, who waived responsibility for the Founder's life if he were to make that trip. But with the favorable opinion—with the gigantic faith—

of those assisting him in the governance of Opus Dei, the Founder traveled to Rome, risking his life, risking everything. And God *"listened to us, and wrote, during those Roman years, another marvelous page of the history of the Work."*

At this point in his life, St. Josemaría fulfilled the words of the Scripture *"virtus in infirmitate perficitur"* ("my strength is made perfect in weakness."), and he commented on these words in a homily: "With faith in the Lord, in spite of our miseries—better, with our miseries—we shall be faithful to our Father God; the divine power will shine, supporting us amidst our weakness."[4]

The Chancellor of the University Alvaro del Portillo,[5] who had accompanied the Founder most closely for almost forty years, wrote:

> Immersed in God, his soul pulled his body in an astonishing way; the spiritual dominated the somatic part that, notwithstanding his mature age, it allowed him to pursue boundless activities that many of you have witnessed... it can't be understood any other way. The doctors who attended to him had told me that the great physical vitality animating him can only be attributed to a supernatural strength. The soul—his love for God and neighbor—gave him that imposing apostolic push which pulls his body—no longer young—upward in such a way that sometimes, he would start one of those catechetical get-togethers very tired—due to lack of sleep—but end it with a desire to start another one immediately for the good of everyone.

[4] "Life of Faith," homily delivered on October 12, 1947 in *Friends of God*, no. 194.

[5] Editor's Note: During this period, Don Alvaro, first successor of St Josemaría, was President General of Opus Dei and Chancellor of the University of Navarre. Cfr. Note 3 of Chapter I.

There was also a great catechetical richness in his homilies, seen in the many analogies he gave between corporal life and the interior life, as when he says: "Prayer becomes continuous, like the beating of our heart, like our pulse."[6]

The apostolate will bring miracles to souls, which he described in effusive lines from his own wonderful experiences and which he compares to the miracles which Jesus and his disciples performed:

> I assure you that God will make us into instruments that can work miracles and, if necessary, miracles of the most extraordinary kind. We will give sight to the blind. Who could not relate thousands of cases of people, blind almost from the day they were born, recovering their sight and receiving all the splendour of Christ's light? And others who were deaf, or dumb, who could not hear or pronounce words fitting to God's children... Their senses have been purified and now they listen and speak as man, not animals. *In nomine Iesu! ("In the name of Jesus")*, his Apostles enabled the cripple to move and walk, when previously he had been incapable of doing anything useful; and that other lazy character, who knew his duties but didn't fulfill them...In the Lord's name, *surge et ambula ("rise up and walk")*.
>
> Another man was dead, rotting, smelling like a corpse: he hears God's voice, as in the miracle of the son of the widow at Naim: " 'Young man, I say to you, rise up' ". We will work miracles like Christ did, like the first Apostles did. Maybe you yourself—and I—have benefited from such wonders. Perhaps we were blind, or deaf, or paralyzed; perhaps we had the stench of death, and the word of Our Lord has lifted us up

[6] *Christ is Passing By, o.c.,* no. 8.

from our abject state.[7]

To study his spiritual itinerary is to comprehend his profound understanding of Jesus Christ and his perception of Jesus as divine Doctor. In his homily on the Eucharist, he refers to the dialogue with Christ during the thanksgiving after Mass; a dialogue which considers him as King, Doctor, Teacher and Friend.

> He is our physician, and he heals our selfishness, if we let his grace penetrate to the depths of our soul. Jesus has taught us that the worst sickness is hypocrisy; the pride that leads us to hide our own sins. We must be totally sincere with him. We have to tell the whole truth, and then we have to say: "Lord, if you will'—and you are always willing—you can make me clean" (Mt 8, 2). You know my weaknesses; I feel these symptoms; I suffer from these failings. We show him the wound, with simplicity, and if the wound is festering, we show the pus too. Lord, you have cured so many souls; help me to recognize you as the divine physician, when I have you in my heart or when I contemplate your presence in the tabernacle.[8]

To use human words for divine realities: isn't this perhaps a correct and fecund way to translate the Mystery of the Incarnation of the Son of God into a language that we can easily comprehend? One will always remember the strength and conviction that made his voice crack, when St Josemaría addressed a huge crowd one bright morning in October 1967 with these words:

[7] *That All May Be Saved* (Homily delivered on April 16, 1964), in Friends of God, o.c., no. 262.

[8] *Christ is Passing By, o.c.,* no. 93.

The University Clinic of Navarre

The Academic clinic, which is the training ground of the medical faculty of the University of Navarre, was founded in 1962 and is considered today as one of the most prestigious and respected hospitals in Europe. The multidisciplinary medical centre has 60 departments in one campus area of over 75 thousand sqm, adjacent to the applied medical research center.

It is equipped with several laboratories and diagnostic centers, ICU and resuscitation for children, a hospital with 350 beds. Each year, the clinic receives more than 140,000 patients coming from 50 countries.

No! We cannot lead a double life. We cannot be like schizophrenics, if we want to be Christians. There is just one life, made of flesh and spirit. And it is this life which has to become, in both soul and body, holy and filled with God."[9]

There is nothing harsh in his spirit nor in his teachings.

But it is necessary to take care of one's health to be able to work intensely and spread the Kingdom of Christ:

"One should strive to take special care of the body so it can be a good instrument of the soul, to avoid extreme physical exhaustion due to circumstances of work or other causes, and which can lead to physical

[9] Editor's Note. This homily, delivered in the Campus of the University of Navarre on October 8, 1967, constitutes one of the clearest syntheses of some essential aspects of the spirit of Opus Dei. It is published with the title *Passionately Loving the World (Conversations) o.c.*, no. 114 ff.

ruin and spiritual dryness which are harmful to one's interior struggle: It is because, I insist, the grace of God counts ordinarily on natural efforts."

Even the pain that is always a blessing from God, one of the treasures of man on earth, and which cannot be despised,[10] must be subjected to a rule of prudence, to a criterion of efficacy.

> "Physical pain, when it can be removed, is removed. There are enough sufferings in life! And when it cannot be taken away, it is offered."

The Founder insisted frequently on the need to devote some time to rest. He recommended that his children must always be in condition to be effective in their professional and apostolic work. He also considered regular medical checkups as particularly necessary. It seems superfluous to say, but he had great confidence in the doctors, whose advice and prescriptions he followed whenever these were needed, and he made his children do the same. In *The Way*, he wrote:

> "Physical collapse. You are worn out... Stop that exterior activity. Rest. Consult a doctor. Obey, and don't worry. You'll soon return to your normal life and, if you are faithful, you'll improve your apostolate."[11]

The Founder possessed an extraordinarily perceptive sensibility: God did not spare him from pains or contradictions. In order to overcome so much stress, in order to keep his serenity and those around him, he learned very soon the efficacy of uniting oneself to the divine designs:

[10] *Ibid*, no. 194.
[11] *The Way*, no. 706.

"The wholehearted acceptance of the will of God is the sure way of finding joy and peace."[12]

That was the prescription he would dispense to those who were stressed, to enable them to recover their serenity and moderate their emotions. Two examples are transcribed below.

In response to someone who asked for words of comfort to alleviate the sorrow of the parents who just lost a son:

> ...tell them that to call it a cross is an offense to the Holy Cross. I do not want that you call crosses whatever gives you pain, because the Cross is the throne where Jesus Christ the High Priest triumphed. Those Christs—rabid, angry—annoy me. The Lord extended his arms with the gesture of a priest and, more than with iron nails, he was nailed to the wood, for Love. He loved us so much, so much that he wanted to suffer much, for each one of us. So he does not seek the grief of those parents.
>
> Allow me to explain. Don't you think I do not cry when the persons whom I love die? During these days I feel uneasy because I have two sons with incurable sicknesses. So I understand, but do not call that a cross, and let them know that they will soon find their son around the corner in no time at all. It is true, life here on earth is a bad night in a bad inn! Life escapes from our hands. Sometimes it is painful to think that way, but it is true. Tell them that they will soon meet their son. In the meantime, they can seek his intercession for all their needs; but they should stop crying. The first tears before the death of a loved one are a gift from God; we

[12] *The Way,* no. 758.

would not be creatures made of flesh and bones if we did not cry. But later, let us not immerse ourselves into a continuing sadness: that would be exaggerating.

On another occasion, the Father gathered his children to ask them to pray for the success of a heart surgery of one of his sons:

> "A few minutes ago, they told me that a brother of yours will undergo an operation. They told me that I can stay for the operation, but I prefer not to go. Unite yourselves to my prayer, to my petition, so that the Lord will cure us. Insist again and again with stubborness, for the Lord will choose to want, always beginning from the fact that we love and accept his most holy Will, though we may find it difficult."

One last manifestation of his love for the ordinary was his acceptance of difficult realities, frequently tough, as a normal ingredient of life. We must receive them initially with naturalness in order to incorporate them afterwards, through Christian optimism, into the *omnia in bonum* which he repeated as an aspiration, an abbreviated formula of the *"diligentibus Deum omnia cooperantur in bonum"* (Rm 8:28). These words are not merely a magic formula to make us serenely endure the harshness of life, but the conviction that God has destined us to conform ourselves to Christ.

> "As long as we walk on this earth, suffering will always be the touchstone of love, sorrows and difficulties—the passing of time that consumes the body and threatens the character with the temptation to bitterness, the seemingly monotonous succession of days that are apparently always the same."[13]

[13] *Christ is Passing By,* no. 24.

Faced with the erosive action of time that passes, we must be determined to conform ourselves to Christ and be faithful to Him:

> "It is difficult to keep this keen sense of loyalty constantly active, as it is always difficult to apply a principle to the changing realities of the contingent world. But it is the best defense against aging of the spirit, hardening of the heart and stiffening of the mind."[14]

I suspect that in these observations lies the reason for his attractive human elegance, inexplicable vigor and, indeed, for the little joke that St. Josemaría made in the last years of his life about his age. When he divided his chronological age by ten and declared with amusement that he was only seven years old, a superficial observer would have only observed something mildly humorous.

> But he had affirmed several years before that ...although I have been around a good many years, when I pray at the foot of the altar "to God who gives joy to my youth", I feel young; and I know that I will never consider myself old. If I keep true to my God, Love will constantly vivify me. My youth will be renewed like that of the eagle.[15]

How interesting it must be to study the reasons for this youthful spirit, for this mature spiritual infancy, above all taking into account that in his youth, he had asked for himself the virtue of dignity: "How hard that young priest—a friend of ours—prayed for it: 'Lord, grant me...eighty years of dignity!'"[16]

[14] *Conversations, o.c.,* no. 1.

[15] "Freedom, a Gift from God" (homily delivered on April 10, 1956), in *Friends of God, o.c.,* no. 31.

[16] *The Way,* no. 72.

"I consider myself so privileged, being granted so many favors."*

Since December 20, 2001, when the Pope John Paul II approved the decree attributing a miracle to Blessed Josemaría Escrivá, the family of Dr. Manuel Nevado has been besieged with phone calls and interviews. It was not in vain that the inexplicable cure of Dr. Nevado prompted the canonization process of the Founder of Opus Dei.

Dr Manuel Nevado, from Almendralejo, a town in the province of Badajoz, Extremadura, is a specialist in General Surgery and Traumatology. His professional work constantly exposes him to the radiation of X-rays, causing his hands to develop early symptoms of radiodermatitis. According to him, it is a progressive disease that is made manifest by wounds and ulcers and does not have any cure except through skin transplant. The worsening of the disease gradually reduces the mobility of the joints, causing severe discomfort. For this reason, he had to abandon his surgical practice.

In November 1992, during a visit to the Ministry of Agriculture in Madrid, he met Luis Eugenio Bernardo, an agricultural engineer. "He noticed my hand was covered with wounds, and he got interested in my sickness. After I told him it did not have any cure, he gave me a prayer card of Blessed Josemaría and advised me to put myself under his protection. I left the office wondering why unusual things were happening to me", he recalls with amusement.

A few days later, he and his wife went to Vienna. In all the churches they visited, they found prayer cards of Blessed Josemaría. "That encouraged me to pray more intensely. Gradually the ulcers on my hands started to heal, until they disappeared completely in fifteen days." In Jan-

*This is the story of Dr. Manuel Nevado, whose "inexplicable" cure prompted the process of canonization of Blessed Josemaría.

uary 1993, after fully recovering the mobility of his limbs, he resumed his surgical work.

Soon the surprising cure of this case of chronic radiodermatitis was announced, and it has been attributed to the intercession of Blessed Josemaría. "As a specialist in medicine I knew the normal evolution of this sickness and its consequences. In fact, I have seen a colleague die of radiodermatitis. Thus, I know that it cannot be cured with conventional treatment."

A process of medical investigations began with trips to Rome to confirm this extraordinary cure. "I remember one of the doctors, who was a dermatologist, was very skeptical. He made a thorough examination and he was impressed with my situation."

In July 1997, the medical consulting group of the Congregation for the Causes of Saints unanimously affirmed that the cure of Dr. Nevado's cancer of serious chronic radiodermatitis in its third stage of irreversibility, was very quick, complete and lasting. It was scientifically inexplicable. After confirming its supernatural character and its causal relationship to Blessed Josemaría's intercession, John Paul II approved a decree recognizing this miracle on December 20, 2001. This opened the way for the canonization, which eventually took place on October 6, 2002.

Dr. Nevado recognized the psychological impact the confirmation of the miracle had on his family. "We were shocked when we heard the news. We didn't know if it was true. In this sense, I consider myself so privileged, being granted so many favors."

From his words we discern that he received the approval of the decree "with respect and surprise." According to Dr. Nevado, "I am a very ordinary person, having dedicated my life to my profession. Since I started my career, I have attended to more than 100,000 patients." This condition of working untiringly despite his sickness, "the sanctification through daily work" seems to have been the deciding factor in the choice of his case as the miracle attributed to Blessed Josemaría for his canonization.